Drama Tweens

Drama Tweens

Engaging the Bible with Younger Adolescents

KATHERINE TURPIN

WIPF & STOCK · Eugene, Oregon

DRAMA TWEENS
Engaging the Bible with Younger Adolescents

Copyright © 2016 Katherine Turpin. All rights reserved. Except for brief quotations in critical publications or reviews, no part of this book may be reproduced in any manner without prior written permission from the publisher. Write: Permissions, Wipf and Stock Publishers, 199 W. 8th Ave., Suite 3, Eugene, OR 97401.

Wipf & Stock
An Imprint of Wipf and Stock Publishers
199 W. 8th Ave., Suite 3
Eugene, OR 97401

www.wipfandstock.com

All biblical quotations taken from the New Revised Standard Version Bible, copyright © 1989, Division of Christian Education of the National Council of the Churches of Christ in the United States of America. Used by permission. All rights reserved.

PAPERBACK ISBN: 978-1-5326-0800-1
HARDCOVER ISBN: 978-1-5326-0802-5
EBOOK ISBN: 978-1-5326-0801-8

Manufactured in the U.S.A.   03/03/17

To the faithful tweens, past and present, of Christ Church
United Methodist in Denver, Colorado.
Your curiosity, courage, and challenge
have made me a better teacher.
Without you, this book would not have been possible.

Contents

Acknowledgments | ix

Part I: Learning the Method
1. Why Create Biblical Dramas with Tweens? | 3
2. Tweens and the Bible | 11
3. Why Interpretive Practice Matters | 20
4. Choosing a Story and Getting Acquainted | 31
5. Creating and Producing the Play | 44

Part II: Sample Dramas
6. In the Green Room: A Post-Pageant Christmas Reflection | 53
7. MST 3000: The Transfiguration | 62
8. Week after Easter: Now What?? | 74
9. Pentecost: The Aftermath | 84
10. Writing Jonah | 93

Bibliography | 107

Acknowledgments

I OWE MY GRATITUDE to several generations of young people of Christ Church United Methodist in Denver, who coauthored this book in many ways through our work together: Clairissa, Mark, Crystal, Eli, Heaven, Verena, Megan, Eric, Bailey, Elizabeth, Selah, Kieran, Bret, Jessica, Miles, Christian, Autumn, Kerith, Jordan, Quinn, Emily, Emelia, and Ben. Their parents and guardians also supported our unconventional approach to Sunday school, providing everything from costume support to dialogue editing. I am also grateful to the pastors of Christ Church throughout the years that these plays were created: Carolyn Waters, Gregory Young, and Eric Strader. They kindly supported and honored the youth in their endeavors, allowing us to take over the sermon on major feast days with our shenanigans. Along with Hebrew Bible scholar and church member Gene Tucker, they also served as resident experts and conversation partners in helping the youth figure out what these texts could mean for us today. My adult colleagues in the classroom, Mark Bramhall, Laurie Fujinami, and Larry and Rebecca Bourgeois, helped hear the young people into voice and dealt with numerous logistical and technical details as we worked to bring their dramas to life. A number of ministers of education and ministry interns also provided support to our work over the years, including Eric Strader, Peggy Stempson, Carissa Fields, Caran Ware Joseph, and Megan Armstrong. I am grateful to be a member of a congregation whose members love their young

Acknowledgments

people, know them by name, and always welcome their contributions to the life of the church.

Parts of this book were written while I was on a research sabbatical supported by the Iliff School of Theology, and parts were written while I was in residence at Ring Lake Ranch in Dubois, Wyoming. Both institutions have been essential to my ongoing development as a scholar and teacher. A section of my Introduction to Christian Religious Education class first heard my musings on creating dramas with tweens and suggested this might be a helpful resource for ministry. Eric Smith and Brian McLaren both graciously read early drafts of this manuscript and provided encouragement and suggestions for improvement that made this a stronger book. Of course, all mistakes that remain are the fault of the author alone.

My work would not be possible without the daily love and household support of my husband and partner in life, Andy Blackmun. My three children, Elizabeth, Christian, and Benjamin, inspire and delight me with their creativity and insight. I first started working with tweens at my church so that they would have a viable youth group to join when they got old enough, and they have all played roles in the dramas contained in these pages.

Part I

Learning the Method

1

Why Create Biblical Dramas with Tweens?

JESUS WAS ONCE TWELVE years old. The Gospel of Luke has a story about Jesus at the stage of life we would now call the tweens, and it is a classic. Jesus is on a journey with his family and an extended party of travelers to Jerusalem for the festival of the Passover. In a move of the independence of this age, he decides to stay in the temple courts, where he dazzles a group of teachers with his curiosity and precocious intelligence. In the very same moment that he amazes the elders, he irresponsibly fails to let his family know of this plan, and they become frantic when they realize after a day's walk that he is not in their travelling party. Upon their return to find him, he is casually indifferent to their panic and questioning about his treatment of them, insisting that it was perfectly predictable for him to have failed to return home with them. His parents are left bewildered by the contradictions in his behavior, a mix of treasuring his unique giftedness and being completely annoyed and put out with him.

Anyone who hangs out with the group of people we now call tweens, younger adolescents just at the cusp of puberty (roughly between the ages of ten and fourteen), can probably recognize the antics of tween Jesus. All that's missing is a smartphone. Young

Part I: Learning the Method

people in this stage of life embody a paradox. In one minute they can astonish with their insight and wit. They have been paying attention to adult conversations, and they can get to the heart of things with an honesty and directness that is refreshingly unstudied. The next moment may include a temper tantrum worthy of a child much younger, complete social ineptitude, or failure to attend to basic responsibilities that have been easily shouldered for the past several years. The self they perform fluctuates and shimmers like a heat mirage off in the distance on a long flat road. The outlines are present, but they are wildly unsteady in how they materialize. Tweens are a challenging population to engage because of this malleability, and yet their changeable nature requires a steady social circle to solidify into mature adulthood. For those interested in the spiritual and faith formation of young people, the tween years present a unique challenge.

When my husband Andy was about twelve years old, a Sunday school teacher showed him that the Christmas story in Matthew never identifies the number of wise persons, only the number of gifts that they bring. Andy thought this information was kind of cool, and he excitedly told his parents what he had learned as they drove home from church. His mother, worried about this potential loss of faith in the truth of the Christian story, told him it would be better to keep believing that there were three kings, just like the hymns said. Years later, after three years of seminary and many years in ministry of various kinds, Andy still remembers this moment as a formative one in his own faith life. Andy's emergent intellectual interest in the Bible and its subsequent parental rebuff has become emblematic to me of a particular transition that congregations struggle to mentor in younger adolescents. When cognitive development that enables critical and comparative thinking begins to emerge in puberty, how do congregations honor that development even as they encourage the growth of faith in their young people?

In the pages to come, I explore a method of engaging with the Bible that allows tweens to begin to get a sense of the broad sweep of stories of the Christian faith tradition found in the Bible.

Why Create Biblical Dramas with Tweens?

As both a professor of religious education in a United Methodist seminary and a volunteer Sunday school teacher in a midsize congregation working with this age group, I have been interested in finding ways of engaging the Christian tradition that make it come alive for young people. The method I describe in this book has helped the young people I work with begin to get a sense of the bigger stories of the Christian faith through deep engagement with one of the smaller stories from the Bible. My hope is that they will begin to understand who God is, why Jesus matters, and who they are called to be through these interactions with an ancient and sometimes puzzling text, even as they are allowed to use all of their emerging capacities of mind to wrestle with the text.

One of the struggles of working with tweens in a mainline or progressive Christian community is that the adults in the community often have mixed feelings about the biblical text and its role in Christian faith. They are sure that the Bible should be an important part of the Christian life, but they have largely rejected it as a source of prooftexting verses or for uncomplicated life advice. And then they get a little stuck. How should this ancient text, with its vastly different culture from the one in which they find themselves, become a source of wisdom for their children? If they don't just use it as an unquestionable source of truth, how should they share it with the next generation in a way that invites growth in spiritual life? In the face of these big questions, I want to share one approach to sharing the Bible with tweens that I have found helpful. In doing so, I hope that I am pointing to these larger questions about how we relate to a religious tradition and share it with the next generation in ways that are neither reductive nor trivializing.

Writing dramas based on longer biblical narratives invites tweens into a form of narrative reasoning that invites connection between their lives and questions and struggles and those of the people depicted in the Bible. At the same time, they are invited into a vibrant historical interpretive tradition that takes the Bible seriously, but not literally, as a source of wisdom for their own faith journeys.

Part I: Learning the Method

How I engage the Bible with tweens is not particularly complicated. We choose a Bible story that is central to Christian belief and practice. Because I worship in a congregation that celebrates the Christian year and sometimes follows the lectionary (a guided set of readings that leads a faith community through major parts of the Bible in a three-year cycle), we often work with stories that are read every year in worship related to Transfiguration, Pentecost, Christmas, Easter, and other annual feast days. Then I work with my band of older elementary kids and middle-schoolers for six to eight weeks during our regularly scheduled Sunday school hour, learning everything we can about this particular story and why people have considered it important to the tradition.

This approach counters the method of many preprinted curricular resources, which often strive for breadth coverage of biblical material, attempting to hit most of the major figures and theological themes over a three- or four-year period. Instead, by going deep with one story, young people in this age group can begin to find the limits of what there is to know about that one passage, a developmentally satisfying approach for this age group. By opening up that one story over many weeks, they can explore how the passage connects to the rest of the book in which it is located and to other stories in other books of the Bible. They can ask questions about the historical setting of the passage and begin to explore cultural and social factors that informed the way it was told to its original audience. They can investigate the symbols and important words and characters that are central to the story. They can find out how other Christians have interpreted the passage throughout history, and why it became important enough to the tradition that we continue to read it today.

If that sounds too sophisticated for the tweens you know, I confess that we also ask what is weird about the text, what puzzles and oddities they wonder about when they read it, and why these inconsistencies were left in the story. In short, we do together slowly what any good preacher would do with a text before she would dare to proclaim it, and in doing so the young people begin to understand the complex ways that biblical texts can and have been interpreted. They become emerging experts on the text, and in the practice come to understand it as their own. This process honors the evolving complexity of their own minds, and it provides an opportunity to see why the Bible is such an interesting text with a long history that belongs to Christians just like them.

After this process of exploration and engagement with the story, we begin to ask questions about what the characters were struggling with in the story, and how those questions and concerns are alive for both the young people and their elders in our congregation. We explore the themes that run through the story, and ask how those same themes and hopes are present in our own community. We bring the concerns and joys of our faith community to the text, and see what lenses these life experiences open for us in the story. We identify the most important insights that they have gained through their process of learning about the text. We find the funny spots in the story, the places that appeal to their adolescent sense of humor. Then we turn these into a short play that we rehearse and present as a sermon for the congregation on the Sunday associated with that text. Easy, right?

The chapters that follow break down this basic process a bit more, exploring why I think this method works particularly well with this age group, ways to choose and explore a biblical story with tweens, and how to go about creating and producing the play. The second half of the book contains plays that I have created with my own little band of tweens at the two-hundred-member Christ Church United Methodist in Denver, Colorado. I include these examples both to demonstrate the kind of learning that can take place and to reassure you that I am not imagining that Pulitzer-quality playwriting will emerge from this process.

Because the process takes a couple of months of an hour a week from start to finish, I use this method once a year in combination with other activities that explore Christian history and theology, spirituality and worship, and service and fellowship during our church's Sunday morning education hour. For instance, the year that we wrote a play related to Christmas, in the early fall we completed a theology unit where we read Roald Dahl's

Part I: Learning the Method

Charlie and the Chocolate Factory as a window into the history of Christian morality plays, the seven deadly sins, liberation theology, and God's preferential option for the poor. In winter and into Lent we did an eight-week unit where we explored different forms of contemplative prayer from centering prayer to praying the Stations of the Cross. After Easter we used an adult curriculum from the Colorado Council of Churches on faithful responses to the immigration crisis and concluded with a service project related to refugee resettlement. In addition, the young people also worshipped with the congregation, participated in fellowship and outreach events with the whole community, and hung out at the occasional young-people-only lock-in or movie night. Together, these units created a set of significant learning experiences with older elementary school children and younger adolescents in a setting with only eight to ten learners across the fourth to eighth grades, staffed entirely by volunteers.

THE GIFT OF THE SMALL COMMUNITY

In my adult life, I have never belonged to a church with enough members to have a youth group bigger than a dozen regular attendees. Although the congregations I have belonged to have loved the youth and children in their midst, they have not been big enough to function as a program-sized congregation. At various points, these churches have lost families to other local churches who were big enough to have paid youth ministers and a youth group of more than thirty members. These smaller congregations have struggled in planning meetings and evangelism efforts with how to have a "viable youth program," which often means attracting enough families with adolescents who can pledge enough money to add to the church budget so they can hire a youth minister to take care of the youth. In the meantime, the handful of adolescents already a part of the congregation have had to wait because there "aren't enough young people" to do youth ministry.

This self-defeating narrative about the makeup of a successful church undercuts the potential strengths and gifts of the smaller congregation. I believe that smaller churches, those with only a handful of youth, are better positioned to do viable youth ministry than big congregations with a hundred youth. By investing in the youth they have, rather than dreaming about and creating programs for the ones they don't, they have the kind of adult-to-young-person ratio of which larger congregations can only dream.

In the last century, children and adolescents have come to spend increasing amounts of time in age-level segregated settings. School settings regularly divide children into groups of only those born in the same twelve-month period. Young people's time outside of school often is spent not with siblings and children of varying ages in the neighborhood, but rather with children of exactly their grade in school in adult–directed and organized activities and care settings. While such segregation allows for organized activities that target the particular cognitive development and physical capabilities of that set of children, it discourages the development of understanding of differences in ability, the empathetic care and responsibility for younger children, and the aspiration to gain the skills and capabilities of the much-admired older kids. Children don't have access to multiple relationships with people of their parents' and grandparents' generations because the adults with them are engaged in organizing and directing group activity without much time to develop individual relationships with children. Our careful attention to the micro-practices of learning in age-segregated settings have created valuable gains in teaching particular skills such as soccer drills and mathematical reasoning. However, these efficiencies gained in large settings that allow for age-segregation also come with costs.

Small congregations often don't have a critical mass of kids in the same age level, making age-segregated educational settings a problem. But such congregations do often have kids who know each other well. These young people have had to entertain each other during congregational and committee meetings. They have adults who know the children and youth by name and are willing to mentor them. Lest you think I am harkening to small towns and rural settings, the congregations I have been most closely associated with are in large urban areas (Atlanta and Denver). One of the gifts of congregations such as these is that they provide a multigenerational setting where relationships develop with others beyond those exactly in one's age and stage of life.

Rather than pining for enough youth for a viable youth program, sometimes meaning a paid young adult who pulls the youth away from the richness of intergenerational community, smaller congregations would be better off working the youth they have been given in an appropriate manner. This perspective is not mine alone. Youth ministry scholars have been wrestling with the fact that membership in a great youth group, ones with lots of youth and regular meetings and events, is no predictive indicator of a healthy adult faith life. In my youth ministry classes at the seminary where I teach, I often find people entering the ministry who say something like, "I never experienced youth ministry. I just hung out with the pastor each week because there were not enough other youth to have a real Sunday school class." Or, "I asked too many questions in Sunday school so I got kicked out of the youth class and joined the adult class. They took me seriously." While these students imagine they didn't experience youth ministry, in fact they were recipients of its best forms. Real relationships with adults just a little further down the path of faith development, who are open to exploring questions alongside them, are a fantastic gift for emerging youthful souls.

The method of biblical engagement explored in this book is ideal with smaller to midsize churches because it can be collaborative and tailored to the people present. Each member knows they make a difference by being there, because no one else could play their role, either in interpreting the text or in representing it to the congregation. My hope for your congregation is that it can embrace the young people present in its midst and invite them to become a part of the grand interpretive tradition of the biblical texts.

2

Tweens and the Bible

ALTHOUGH I HAVE INCLUDED older teenagers in creating plays based on Bible stories, I believe this method is most developmentally appropriate for tween learners. By tweens, I mean those in the later elementary school years through early adolescence. This period corresponds biologically to the transition through the initial stages of puberty for most girls and boys in developed nations. Socially, this group often is still connected to the congregation, but is beginning to ask different questions than their younger elementary peers. Because they are in the midst of major cognitive and physical transformations, they can demand a steady emotional presence in their leaders. However, if you are willing to be delighted and curious about these transformations rather than intimidated by them, tweens can absolutely be the most fun age group in the church to work with. They are smart, quick, honest, lively, and creative.

COGNITIVE TRANSFORMATION

Cognitively, emerging critical and abstract thinking skills invite young people of these ages to begin to engage differently with Bible stories. While a seven- or eight-year-old is happy to hear and accept a story as story, as children grow older they begin to ask interesting questions about how things work. They start to use their critical reasoning skills and experience to begin to ask different questions about what they are learning in church: "Why didn't the lions eat the antelopes on the ark?" "How can somebody live to be that old?" "I prayed and prayed for my mother, so why wasn't her multiple sclerosis healed?" "Is the only way to the Father really through Jesus? What about my friend Sarah, who is Jewish?"

As these questions emerge, sometimes adults working with young people begin to worry that such questioning will lead to a loss of faith. However, honoring these questions by inviting young people into more grown-up thinking about their experiences with God and their faith tradition helps them to understand what it means to love God with their heart, soul, *and* mind. They are ready to talk about things like the difference between poetry, letters, history, and other biblical genres. They are reading long novels in other parts of their lives, and are ready to reason narratively with bigger stories with nuanced and realistic characters. In short, they are on the cusp of transitioning out of childhood, out of childlike reasoning, and they need the support to begin to apprehend their faith in more complex ways suitable to their adolescent and adult years.

During these years the brain begins an extended process of transformation, shedding excess neurons and refining which kinds of thinking need to be carried on into adulthood. Therefore, giving tweens practice with their advanced thinking in relationship to their spiritual life is essential. They are entering a "use it or lose it" period with their brains, so even though the going can be a little tough in the transition, this is a particularly critical time for educational interventions. Tweens are beginning to use more complex forms of reasoning and thinking, but at the same time the transition to a fully developed prefrontal cortex, with its capacity for long-term planning and fully integrative thinking between emotion and cognition, has only begun. This process takes between ten and twelve years to complete. Finding ways to allow them to connect these emerging cognitive skills with their faith and spirituality allows them to grow into more mature forms of adult faith.

Tweens need adults ready to dive into engaging the faith tradition in more complex ways alongside them. In her book about cognitive science and the teenage brain, Barbara Strauch reminds parents and teachers of young people in this transition period that they sometimes need adults to serve as a surrogate prefrontal cortex to help this brain development happen.[1] A delicate balance must be maintained between providing tweens options and paths that can be taken and allowing them to begin to make choices that allow their emergent capacities to be activated. What tweens often get instead are adults who can tolerate and perhaps even enjoy their squirrelly energy, but who may not be willing or able to engage these critical emergent questions of faith with them. Finding adult mentors who are excited about these signs of more complex thinking and who want to engage those difficult questions serves the tween well.

SOCIAL DEVELOPMENT OF THE SELF

Adult mentors are also essential because younger adolescents are becoming highly attuned to the relationships and social dynamics around them. They are beginning to understand that the way they experience themselves internally is not exactly the way that other people experience them from the outside. Faith development expert James Fowler calls this skill the development of mutual critical perspective taking, captured in his catchy couplet: "I see you seeing me. I see the me I think you see.[2]" The awareness that other people have a different perspective leads to an increasing sense that their own identity is a performance with an audience of the people around them. This novel experience often leads tweens and early adolescents to feel as though everyone is watching them all the time. While many adults interpret this as narcissism or

---

1. Strauch, *Primal Teen*, 206.
2. Fowler, *Stages of Faith*, 153.

"thinking the world revolves around them," in fact it is a developmental achievement of increased awareness about the different perspectives of others.

This new world of understanding that others see you differently than you see yourself launches an identity construction project that often involves many fits and starts. As educational psychologists Michael Nakkula and Eric Toshalis note, adolescents are driven to be great experimenters as they engage the process of constructing their own identity in relationship to those around them.[3] This leads to the clowning and low-brow humor that often marks this age—I can make people laugh! It also leads to the painful sense of being on stage all the time, an experience that sometimes causes tweens to hide behind rigid conformity to peer trends in clothing or go along with the socially powerful in their group even against their better judgment. When we overemphasize the importance of peer relationships in younger adolescence and lump a bunch of these experimenters together without much adult interaction, we leave them to try to create a sense of who they are and what is important in the midst of other humans who are not very good at processing emotional and social cues. To link them with adult mentors allows them to have a more experienced and stable audience that responds to the experimentation with a steadiness that offers them a better north star around which to orient themselves.

While adult mentors are absolutely crucial to tweens in this time period, serving in this capacity can be a bit of a thankless task. All of this social learning and cognitive transformation is going on, but tweens are often unable to narrate their own experience of the construction project in motion reliably to people who work with them, so it is difficult to track the wonder of this transformation. Some tweens turn inward to avoid putting themselves out there and looking foolish, and do not talk much at all about what is happening with them. Some early adolescents talk constantly, but not about things that matter most. Being an adult working with young people at this stage is often an experience of great mystery. Sometimes it is difficult to see what impact you are having on

---

3. Nakkula and Toshalis, *Understanding Youth*, 4.

young people, and they may not notice or remember the way you are shaping and contributing to their sense of self.

By providing a shared project for adults and tweens to work on together, creating a drama provides an opportunity to talk about faith, meaning, and shared commitments and to draw on strengths of both groups while focusing on a third thing rather than directly on either the adult or tween. The drama aspect also mirrors the experience of feeling on stage all the time for younger adolescents as they begin to realize that they are performing a self for a wider social audience that reads them externally. The public performance provides an opportunity for the congregation to see the youth in a positive role and connect with them in a constructive setting, which counteracts the often negative stereotypes that adults have about teenagers.

DESIRE FOR COMPETENCY

When developmental psychologist Erik Erikson described the developmental task for older elementary-aged children, he named the struggle as developing a sense of industry instead of one of inferiority. The virtue that he believed emerged from this stage is *competence*, the ability to perform tasks valued by one's community with an adult level of skill.[4] This approach to ministry leverages tween desires to demonstrate competency in performance in order to gain biblical and theological literacy. Going deep with a single story and committing a long period of time to it serves tweens well by allowing them to become experts in the stories they choose, to know everything the adults in their community know, and more, about that one story. Youth leaders commonly want to keep switching things up so that they do not get bored, but this constant transition actually can be counterproductive. Tweens long to demonstrate their capacity to know something and to be able to do it as well as the adults around them. This process gives them an opportunity to shine in the church with their emergent capacities

---

4. Erikson, *Insight and Responsibility*, 122.

for playful humor, intelligence, and knowledge of at least one piece of the Christian tradition.

Adults in faith communities recognize the emerging gifts of young people, often through the celebration of victory in swim meets, band competitions, or academic achievements. Creating a biblical drama allows young people to demonstrate competence with the church's own story, and in doing so to give a gift back to their community. Providing a solid interpretation of a beloved (or unfamiliar or strange) story puts tweens in a position of leadership of the community, creating an artifact valued by the adults around them, while satisfying their desire to be competent. They relish the experience of not just needing to be entertained, but rather finding that they can create something valuable for the community. Of course, there are many other ways we can and should help tweens to shoulder responsibility and take on tasks that matter to the community beyond the interpretation of biblical stories, but biblical interpretation is one identifying marker of Christian faith.

CULTURAL CONGRUENCE

In the United States, tweens are growing up in a cultural setting that focuses strongly on performance as a site for personal expression and identity development. Television reality shows such as *The Voice* and *Dancing with the Stars* as well as homemade YouTube channels are a daily experience valorizing performance as a desirable form of adolescent and young adult expression. Many school assignments now focus more on project and performance tasks, as educators increasingly understand the value of personal integration and reconstruction of knowledge in these educational processes. For these reasons, a performance-based exploration of the Bible fits culturally with what adolescents are experiencing through mass media, social media, and the schools they attend.

The creation of their own play allows tweens to put the biblical tradition into their own language. The artistic license of dramatic form means that some snark is allowed in their interaction with the tradition, but the intended congregational audience helps reinforce the idea that both in church and online they have an audience beyond their peers. The flattening of authority that is common in online environments is modeled in this process, as young people are granted the opportunity to be expert in at least this one text, and to engage it on their own terms. Additionally, the extended focus on one text over time allows for spotty attendance at church while still having a chance to really dig into a biblical text and come to learn it as one's own. Given the reality of many tween lives, being shuffled between parental work schedules, multiple blended families, and extracurricular activities, a method that takes this sporadic attendance into mind is important. All of these characteristics give this approach to Bible study a cultural congruence that makes it motivating and engaging for young people.

OWNING THE STORIES

Religious educator and youth ministry expert Michael Warren once noted that young people need to move from house guest to family member in their relationship to the church and their knowledge of the Christian tradition.[5] In using this metaphor, he emphasizes the need for young people to begin to own the stories of the tradition as their own and to develop both familiarity with them and the capacity to interpret them. Recently, sociologist Christian Smith has lamented the reality that the average US Christian teenager has only marginal religious literacy with the big themes and doctrines of their own tradition. In a study of nearly three thousand teenagers nationwide, he found that young people from the historically mainline Protestant traditions struggled most to communicate the heart of their tradition.[6]

To spend time with one story and to enter it deeply enough to interpret it for their congregation invites tweens into the stories of their own tradition, to move beyond religious illiteracy and to begin to function as a family member in the household of faith.

---

5. Warren, *At This Time, in This Place*, 77.
6. Smith and Denton, *Soul Searching*, 137.

By gaining experience with ethical practices of the interpretation of the biblical text, these stories begin to have a different kind of relevance beyond application in an interpersonal arena. In this process, tweens come to know these stories as *their* stories to understand and interpret for the community. Finally, forming deep connections with the nuances of biblical narratives provides building blocks for the stories of their own faithful journey—gifts from the tradition to the faithful imagination, as theologian Horace Bushnell named it over a century ago.[7]

PROBLEM- OR INQUIRY-BASED LEARNING

Framing the encounter with the biblical text in terms of creating a drama to share in worship places this approach in what educators call problem-based or inquiry-based learning. The problem that tweens face that must be solved is something like: we have to (1) create a good play that (2) we find funny but also (3) treats the biblical text with respect, in which (4) everyone can be involved and (5) utilize their unique strengths and limitations, and that (6) interprets the text with significance for the congregation and (7) costs almost no money to produce. These seven limiting conditions, which may seem a bit daunting, actually breed creativity. The challenge of the problem and the need to produce something at the end for the people they care about create motivation to engage in the process and to work hard on it.

Often Sunday school lessons lack this kind of investment and challenge. They don't demand much of the participants, and they don't invite them to rise to any sort of challenge besides staying awake on a Sunday morning. The crafts and artistic projects created in Sunday school are generally designed to be completed in fifteen minutes and be ultimately disposable—if they do not end up discarded under the church pews before the morning is over.

---

7. Bushnell, *Building Eras in Religion*, 249–85. Both James Fowler and Sharon Daloz Parks pick up on Bushnell's idea of the biblical tradition as a gift to the faithful imagination, and it is in their work where I first came across the phrase.

Problem-based inquiry has been a longstanding staple in educational theory because it draws on human motivations for creativity and ingenuity to promote the hard work of learning. However, creating a drama only remains a challenge if the leaders of the process are willing to let their participants struggle and even fail at the task. Rescuing or doing the work for the tweens undercuts the challenge aspect that is motivating in the process.

If the young people are allowed to struggle and to triumph in creating something of value to themselves and to the community, they walk away with many desirable outcomes. They gain familiarity with some of the major stories of the faith tradition, practice in historical and literary interpretation of the Bible, skills in interpreting a text for a particular community, skills in public presentation and leadership, and an increased sense of teamwork and belonging in the church. Happily, they gain these benefits without knowing they are doing it! The experience of learning about the story and creating the play is fun, engaging, and challenging. They understand that something is at stake in their work, and they feel loved and connected to their community and their tradition.

You may decide to perform dramas written by other people, including the ones at the end of this book. I want to encourage you to try writing your own with your young people, and the following chapters will explain the process so that you can do it. First, I want to explore a bit more why learning skills of biblical interpretation is so important for tweens as a part of their faith development.

3

Why Interpretive Practice Matters

IN CHARLES FOSTER'S BOOK *Educating Congregations*, he names five critical flaws in the church's educational vessel that have emerged over the last century: the loss of communal memory; the irrelevance of the Bible for contemporary life because of the way we teach it; the subversion of educational goals for consumer experiences at church; the continuing cultural captivity of Christian education, including its participation in racism and sexism; and profound changes in the structure of family, school, and media.[1] Each of these issues has challenged the local congregation's ability to teach the Bible to the next generation. The loss of communal memory means that many congregations do not have adults who are prepared to help respond to serious questions of faith and to model Christian discipleship. Decades of teaching the Bible as an instruction book, or with isolated verses as mottos or memory pieces, have left the depth of its wisdom untapped by many lay people. Christian communities have become one option among many for programmatic and enrichment experiences for children and youth, and sometimes a suspect option because of clergy sex abuse scandals, evidence of hypocrisy on issues of racial and gender

---

1. Foster, *Educating Congregations*, 22.

inclusion in leadership, and a sense of cultural conservatism that seems out of touch with everyday reality for many persons.

In response to these concerns about how Christian education is failing to pass wisdom on to the next generations, Foster advocates an "event-centered" model of education, where the seasonal, occasional, and life-cycle events of the congregation drive faith development.[2] By focusing on the production of a shared moment of congregational experience, here represented by a drama presented in worship, participants engage in preparation, participation, and reflection on that event. These three phases provide many opportunities for gaining knowledge, experience, and reflective capacities central to what we mean by education. Rather than a series of disconnected lessons in a classroom, the learning is linked to an event that young people share with others. Creating biblical dramas links the preparation, participation, and reflection of the event with an experiential connection to interpretative practice, or what Bible scholars call exegesis.

There is a link between the way we read the Bible and the formation of the Christian self. Many teenagers, and indeed many adults, only have an experience of reading the Bible as an answer book (the positive take) or a source for proof-texting (a negative take). For example, in some Bibles designed for life application, you will find indexes that read: "Do you struggle with eating too much? Read Proverbs 23: 20–21." Or, "Here is a list of verses that you can read if you are seeking comfort in times of trouble." Or, "Read Micah 6:8 if you want to know the kind of person God wants you to be." They might have received a greeting card for eighth grade graduation with this Bible verse: "For surely I know the plans I have for you, says the Lord, plans for your welfare and not for harm, to give you a future with hope" (Jeremiah 29:11).

This interpretive strategy is well meaning. On the one hand, teachers and other adults working with teenagers want to help them to connect the sacred text with the important events and struggles of their lives. They want tweens to have concrete tokens of their importance to God and Christ's importance to them by

---

2. Ibid., 37–50.

Part I: Learning the Method

having "memory verses" that connect to their daily lives and become so much a part of their formation of self that they are anchors in the midst of difficulty. Progressive and mainline Christians may struggle with the proof-texting of their Christian brothers and sisters, but they also have a hard time articulating constructively what a different reading and interpretive practice might be. Sometimes they simply replace the "God has a plan for your lives" personal piety verses with "God wants justice for the oppressed" verses instead of developing a different way to read Scripture and make meaning with it.

This kind of reading of the Bible often takes a particular verse completely out of its original context in the Scriptures. As an example, the verse "But as for me and my household, we will serve the Lord" (Joshua 24:15b) is often used with young people (and on cross-stitch samplers and greeting cards) as a positive encouragement to be a godly person and/or family. But if you read the book of Joshua, you come to realize that this is a divisive moment in Israel's history, a demand for loyalty in the form of rejecting people of other religious groups in the midst of genocidal wars. It was not the most shining moment in God's interreligious peacemaking. Another more comical example is a recent Internet meme showing a daily devotional calendar with the verse "All these things will I give thee, if thou wilt fall down and worship me," from Matthew 4:9 in the King James Version. Sounds great, until you realize that this is not proof of the correctness of the prosperity gospel but instead the words of Satan when he is tempting Jesus in the wilderness. This kind of inspirational cherry-picking of verses dishonors the text by chopping it into little bits and distorting the meaning of the verses. What was a temptation from Satan for Jesus becomes a promise from God for prosperity in exchange for loyal devotion in calendar form.

When younger adolescents start to encounter the Bible more fully and discover the contradictions that exist within it, they can get confused as to how it is a truthful book that might be authoritative in their own walk of faith. If their primary encounters with Scripture have been in decontextualized bite-size chunks, they do not have the tools they need to engage it faithfully. Do we "beat our plowshares into swords and our pruning hooks into spears" as commanded in Joel 3:10, or "beat our swords into plowshares and our spears into pruning hooks" as is promised in Isaiah 2:4? When adolescents experience the Bible used as a weapon in church fights or against the full inclusion of LGBTQ persons, they can get cynical and begin to think that you can make the Bible say anything. This stance on the biblical text is not helpful to their understanding of God or their own spiritual journey. Helping adolescents become sophisticated interpreters of the Bible can heal this disillusionment by working alongside them so they learn that the Bible can help us connect with God only to the degree that it is interpreted skillfully and with the inspiration of the Holy Spirit. Learning to interpret the text is part of growing into adult faith, and it takes practice.

A GLIMPSE INTO THE HISTORY OF BIBLICAL INTERPRETATION

In an age where literal interpretation of Scripture is a fundamental commitment held up by many individuals, groups, and institutions as the most faithful way to adhere to God's desires for our lives, it is difficult to remember that the history of biblical interpretation all the way back to the writing of the New Testament understands the literal interpretation of Scripture as only the most basic and spiritually immature way of understanding the Bible. Both Jewish and Christian interpreters of Scripture believed that the Bible held many meanings within it, understanding that faithful interpretation required study, attention to the whole of the Scriptures, and divine revelation as part of the interpretive practice.

Places of contradiction, repetition, and unseemly behavior by important patriarchs were all sources of confusion for early Jewish interpreters of the Torah (the first five books of the Hebrew Bible or Christian Old Testament). An entire tradition of scholarly argument and debate about these troubling passages contributed to the development of Jewish interpretive tradition, some of which is captured in the Talmud. Precisely because the rabbis thought that

Part I: Learning the Method

everything in Scripture was inspired and intentional, they worked hard to make sense of the contradictions and concerning elements of the texts they loved. This tradition understood there to be multiple levels of meaning in any biblical text, including meaning in the gaps in the text that were essential to engage in order to learn from the Scriptures.

Sandy Sasso, the first female rabbi in the Reconstructionist tradition of Judaism and author of many children's books, teaches and writes about the ancient practice of *midrash*. In this practice, early interpreters filled in the gaps found in the biblical writings, adding details, connections, character names, and motivations to make sense of contradictions and omissions in the text. For example, her children's book *Noah's Wife: The Story of Namaah* picks up on the fact that the biblical character is nameless, and adds an entire task for her given by God to bring all of the seeds and roots of plants so that plants as well as animals could be re-established on the earth.[3] In creating this story, Sasso is confidently making up story material that is in the spirit and faithful lineage of the tradition. Sasso reminds us: "Midrash gives us permission to do just that, not only to be descendants but to become ancestors who bequeath our spiritual quest to future generations. We approach this task with a deep sense of humility, honoring its ancient origins and layers upon layers of understanding.[4]" It is this kind of confident interpretive engagement with the tradition that the practice of creating biblical dramas encourages.

Early interpreters who read the Bible closely understood that there needed to be more complex strategies of making meaning from the biblical texts than the plain meaning of the text.[5] In both Jewish and Christian interpretation of Scripture, the text had a life of its own that required careful tending and engagement to begin to discern the wisdom within it. In fact, the face-value meaning of

---

3. Sasso, *Noah's Wife*.
4. Sasso, *God's Echo*, 25.
5. For a helpful description of the history of biblical interpretation for lay people, see Viviano, "Senses of Scripture," found at http://www.usccb.org/bible/national-bible-week/upload/viviano-senses-scripture.pdf.

the words on the page were considered only the most basic level of understanding. The fullest meaning of the text could not be printed on tear-off pages or just memorized; it required faithful study and wrestling with the meaning of Scripture to allow it to bestow a blessing on its readers.

In the third century, Origen advocated for multiple layers of interpretation in Scripture. He had many ways of describing these layers, including the historical, mystical, literal, moral, and allegorical, but he most often pointed to the literal meaning and the spiritual meaning of the text.[6] In speaking of these different meanings that were able to be discerned, he often was pointing to the skill and spiritual wisdom of the reader as an interpreter. Augustine, too, "read Scripture not merely as containing a specific truth, but as generating many truths," believing that the strength of Scripture lay in its fullness to offer many truths.[7] In the late fourth century, John Cassian proposed a fourfold sense of Scripture that included its literal/historical meaning, its allegorical meaning, its tropological meaning, and its anagogical meaning. These latter three are technical forms of the "spiritual senses" of reading Scripture, which look to how it works to describe the life of faith beyond the literal sense of the story on the page. As Cassian proposed,

> The one Jerusalem can be understood in four different ways, in the historical sense as the city of the Jews, in allegory as the Church of Christ, in anagoge as the heavenly city of God "which is the mother of us all" (Gal 4:26), in the tropological sense as the human soul.[8]

As indicated in Cassian's quote, many of these different kinds of interpretations of the historical city of Jerusalem in spiritual terms are already happening by the time the New Testament is written, as these new writings interpreted the Hebrew Scriptures in light of the community's experiences with Jesus. Other church leaders and

---

6. Martin, *Pedagogy of the Bible*, 50.
7. Ibid., 57.
8. Cassian, *Conferences*, 160.

scholars continued to refine this fourfold interpretation schema over the centuries.

As the Age of Enlightenment progressed and the Protestant reformers began to engage biblical interpretation, they became more suspicious of alleghorical, tropological, and anagogical readings of Scripture. Both a literal and a historical reading of Scripture re-emerged in importance in this period, as the study of archeology and science began to change how we understand the nature of history. However, the spiritual and moral interpretive work of reading Scripture never was erased, even as in the subsequent centuries modern historical-critical methods began to dominate biblical interpretation in a quest to better understand the original intent of authors and the understanding of their audiences as central to biblical interpretation.

Over the centuries, succeeding generations have brought their interpretive practices to the biblical text. Enslaved persons of African descent in the United States took images of Scripture and wove them into images of hope and strength in spiritual songs that built on their stories. In the sixties and seventies of the last century, those involved in liberation movements for the underclass in Latin American countries began to read the Bible with their own experiences seeking God's advocacy on behalf of the oppressed. Feminist scholars scoured the Scriptures trying to hear the stories of unnamed women and to undo histories of interpretation that suppressed the role of women in religious movements. Academic Bible scholars have studied literary genres, reader response, and comparative literature from the same time period and region of the world as the biblical texts. Basically, any form of analysis and interpretation used with literature has been used in biblical interpretation. Over time, generations of faithful people have struggled to make sense of their own experiences in light of scriptural texts, wrestling with them to seek a word for their lives.

TWEENS AND NARRATIVE REASONING

So how do we invite these emerging tween minds into the time-honored work of wrestling with Scripture to discover its many meanings in their lives? Many church educational resources begin with life issues and use select Bible verses to Christianize what are basically popular psychological approaches to topics such as bullying, stress over school success, or other struggles. I believe that working with an issue a week as a way to connect the Bible with tween lives falls short of what is needed for their moral and spiritual development. This reading method positions the Bible as a backup external authority to their own experience rather than a central place of investigation and imaginative exploration into the heart of God.

In his book on teaching the Bible to people in seminaries, New Testament scholar Dale Martin explores how it might be to drop the idea of the Bible as a rule book or blueprint and instead imagine the Scriptures as

> a space we enter, rather than a bookish source for information. . . .[W]e should imagine that when we enter the space of Scripture by either reading it alone or hearing it read in church we are entering a space where our Christian imaginations may be informed, reshaped, even surprised by the place Scripture becomes for us.[9]

If we imagine the Bible as a cathedral, when we enter into it and look around, some places are exquisitely beautiful, while others are dusty, lifeless corners. For tweens to gain the inspiration and beauty of the Scriptures, they first have to have a chance to explore the cathedral, to enter into the stories and poke around a little bit on the terms of the story itself. Instead of grabbing hold of a text that they know has been interpreted to say a particular thing, they wander in and see what there is to see, to be inspired by, to wonder about, and to explore.

Think about the way that tweens read the Harry Potter books, or Rick Riordan's various series based on ancient mythology, or

---

9. Martin, *Pedagogy of the Bible*, 101.

the other novelized series that they love. They just dive into the world and play along with its rules and limitations. In doing so, they are inspired by Hermione's brilliance and courage; they feel connection for Ron's bumbling form of loyalty; they are captured by Percy's struggles to connect to his distant father from whom he inherited both extraordinary power and a giant mysterious hole in his family. They get to know the characters, they live through their struggles vicariously, and along the way they learn about courage, commitment, loyalty, friendship, and vocation. Contemporary research demonstrates that reading literary fiction builds skills for empathy and entering into the perspectives of those who are quite different from us.

Researcher of children's spirituality Rebecca Nye advocates that children be allowed to find in the spaces of the Bible opportunities to enjoy being themselves with God in their "own native languages of play and story":

> This can mean all sorts of things, including the freedom simply to enjoy the stories for their own sake, allowing their archetypal themes of freedom, loss, love, identity and so on to resonate intuitively, playfully, often without words, with the children's sense of these themes in their own lives.[10]

It is this kind of engagement with Scripture that best forms an identifying connection with the scriptural texts. This form of narrative reasoning and engagement is quite different from "having a memory verse to hang on to." The ability to enter into a narrative world is particularly strong in tween readers, whose imaginations are supple and whose thirst for the heroic is particularly high. Because of their skills in narrative reasoning, I have often taught tweens in a book club format using stories and characters they are much more deeply related to in order to leverage their narrative engagement for Christian formation, making links back to Christian theology and concepts and eventually back to the religious narratives found in the Bible. For example, Lois Lowry's Newbery

---

10. Nye, *Children's Spirituality*, 35.

Medal-winning novel *The Giver* allowed us to have conversations on what it means to have a vocation as we explored how Jonas was chosen as the keeper of memory for his community, as well as conversations about trying to solve issues like racism and sexism by eliminating sexual passion and the ability to see color.

Igniting this capacity for narrative exploration with the Bible can be more difficult. The Bible is an ancient text written by and for people who understood life quite differently than we do. Often the emotional motivation of characters is left unexplored in biblical narratives, and the symbols and customs that were important to the initial audience for the text are often obscure for contemporary readers. But, there are still traces of human emotion and motivation that tweens can connect to if they work with a text long enough and are given permission to use their imaginations to engage it.

Let me share an example of the Christian formation created by this kind of narrative engagement. I had a friend who studied the Hebrew Bible (Old Testament) at the doctoral level. She grew to love the text so much she wondered if she might convert to Judaism. One day she was driving to school when she saw a group of day laborers standing in a parking lot, waiting to be picked up for work. It was past nine in the morning, so she knew their chances of getting chosen for work was dwindling as the sun grew higher in the sky. In that moment, she realized why she was irreversibly Christian. Immediately what jumped into her mind was the parable of the laborers in the vineyard from Matthew's Gospel. She knew that the Christian stories from the Gospels were so much a part of her identity from her childhood formation that she would always be at least partly Christian. It is this kind of ownership of and imaginative connection to the stories of the text that I think is important: to know the stories so deeply that they color the way that you see and interpret the world.

Creating a drama from a biblical story is like engaging in a form of *midrash*. Tweens are writing into the gaps of the text, exploring the motivations of the characters and the unseemly actions of people or God, just like their ancestral interpreters in the

Part I: Learning the Method

Jewish and Christian traditions. As an adult leader, writing a form of biblical fan fiction may feel sacrilegious, like you are just making stuff up that should not have a deep relationship to the Scriptures. However, this work allows tweens to leverage their playfulness to really see what is in the text and to connect with it on a personal and imaginative level.

My goal in this process of play writing is to help them explore the broad trajectories of the stories in the Bible so that they can connect with the bigger arcs using their capacity for narrative reasoning. To do so, we work not just with single stories such as a particular event or parable, but with larger chunks of the text, often through the lens of an initial story. For example, there are what are sometimes called the cycles or novellas in the Old Testament, such as the Elijah cycle in 1 Kings or Joseph's story in Genesis. This can also be an entire biblical book, as with Ruth, Esther, or Jonah. In the New Testament this process requires looking at a character across several chapters, books, or letters, such as the disciples trying to figure out what to do next after the crucifixion of their friend and leader.

Another alternative to writing your own plays about these texts is to perform already existing plays inspired by biblical texts, such as Madeleine L'Engle's *The Journey with Jonah*, Tom Key's adaptation of Clarence Jordan's *The Cotton Patch Gospels*, the Schwartz/Tebelak musical *Godspell*, or even the plays at the end of this book. These plays have recreated the motivations, the connections needed, for modern readers of stories, and performing them provide moments of being able to dive into questions of interpretation, meaning making, and the relevance of these stories. However, I think in this particular era the creation and production of cultural objects to share is highly valued. Writing biblical dramas is a good way to practice being in community while becoming deeply engrossed in these stories and learning how people have made them relevant. In the next chapter, we will explore how to find a big-enough story for tweens to explore.

4

Choosing a Story and Getting Acquainted

BECAUSE WRITING A PLAY requires spending a long time with a particular biblical story, choosing a big-enough story to warrant the time is important. What do I mean by a "big-enough" story? There are several reasons a story could qualify for that designation. Sometimes stories are big enough because we read them regularly in the church as part of the Christian liturgical year on Christmas, Pentecost, or Maundy Thursday. Because they have become a part of the formational strategy of the larger church, they are worth taking the time to explore more closely. Each time the story comes around in the Christian year, the young people have an instant connection with it. It has become their story.

Some stories typify big themes found in the Bible, such as the exodus from Egypt, the experience of exile, or visions of salvation. Some stories are linked to big characters in the Bible whose stories get riffed on in stories that were written later. Some are stories that have life resonance with tweens because they focus on sibling rivalry, getting into trouble, or being required to do stuff that you don't want to do by an authority figure. All of these qualify stories as big enough to engage in with a drama-writing adventure.

Part I: Learning the Method

As an example, let's explore why the transfiguration is such a great story to do this. This story shows up in the three Synoptic Gospels (Mark 9:1–8; Matthew 17: 1–13; Luke 9:28–36). To be honest, I first included the transfiguration story because, in a church with lectionary-based preaching, it comes every year just before the beginning of Lent, and it is a weird story. Jesus goes up on a mountain with his disciples, who fail entirely at being good companions to him on the way, Moses and Elijah show up, and then Jesus' head lights up like a lightbulb. So, what does a tween take from that hot mess? At first my choice was pragmatic: if we work on that story, they will find it familiar and homey when it comes up every year. Plus, my pastor at the time hated preaching it, so he was glad to pass it on for the youth to preach on that Sunday.

Why does this story come up every year in the liturgical calendar? The practice of Christian timekeeping was a formative practice in the church. The seasons allow church members in a year to relive the important rhythms of Jesus' life, death, and resurrection and other key ideas in the theology of the church. Transfiguration comes up every year because it is an essential story about the nature of the Messiah and his continuous relationship with the Law and the Prophets. So, by trying to perform that one story, we had an excuse to dive into the Elijah stories. Elijah serves as a representative prophet and one story of the hope for a messiah that early followers of Jesus turned to for understanding of their leader. We also explored the giving of the law, one divine salvation strategy from the stories of Moses. The story also includes all the fun of the disciples misunderstanding this great teacher and having the experience but missing the meaning of it. Plus, it contains big weird dramatic elements. No wonder they chose to put it in the lectionary every year just before Lent! This one story calls up major themes and characters of the Hebrew Bible and helps explain the significance of Jesus by using them. This is what I mean by one smaller story capturing the bigger stories across books of the Bible and the large spans of time in which they were originally written.

You will notice that many of the other big-enough stories that we take on in the representative dramas in the final section of this book are about the nature and person of Jesus. In many ways this occurred for us because they were tied to the Christian year. They become relevant not in snippets, but in the relatability of the characters, who are also trying to figure out what is going on with this whole Jesus thing. By becoming emerging experts on these stories that come around every year, young people begin to feel more connected in worship when these feast days come around again. They are better equipped to understand the symbolism and nuance of hymns that draw on these stories in imagery and shorthand reference. They become more of a member of the household of faith and less a stranger in a strange place in communal worship.

As a side note, this liturgical strategy could be an entry into studying church history as well. For example, an All Saints play could be the opportunity to explore the church tradition of naming saints and a chance to get to know some of the big figures in church history, such as St. Francis, Teresa of Avila, Dorothy Day, or Martin Luther King Jr. For example, you might set the play in a mythical Saintly Processing Center, where St. Francis, Dorothy Day, Hildegard von Bingen, and Martin Luther greet the recently dead Jenny, who doesn't see herself as a saint. This would give an opportunity to explore the strange and exotic lives of many of those the church has named as saints (again, a classic formational experience), but also to question what it means to be a saint in traditions that understand this experience as reserved for all the faithful, not just a chosen few.

Teaching the lives of the saints is a classic formational strategy because younger adolescents appear to be hardwired to look up to heroes as a part of their own identity exploration. Traditions as diverse as the Roman Catholic Church (Alban Butler's *The Lives of the Saints*) and the Mennonites (Thieleman Van Bragt's *Martyrs Mirror*) used the lives of the saints as inspiration for young people to live into their faith more fully. Along this line, exploring the big characters in the Bible such as Job, Paul, Deborah, Joseph, Adam and Eve, Ruth, John the Baptist, Elijah, and Moses can link to the idea of the heroic, but also give tweens the opportunity to see them as realistic human beings who struggled to be faithful and not just as idealized people of faith.

Despite my insistence that life lessons aren't the best way to connect to biblical stories, I do believe that life resonance is one way that tweens relate to Bible stories. For example, many of the big stories in the Bible have to do with sibling rivalry: Jacob and Esau, Cain and Abel, Joseph and his brothers, Mary and Martha, Rachel and Leah, James and John. It might be fun to have a play set in a sibling rivalry therapy group, engaging all of their stories alongside a contemporary sibling pair from the congregation. Many of the texts of disciples resonate with being a student of someone you don't quite understand, so that all of the places where the disciples fail to comprehend what is happening could come together into a summer school remedial classroom for disciples who failed the first time around. Other Bible stories are about people having to do stuff they just don't want to do, like Moses getting sent to Pharoah, Jonah getting sent to Ninevah, the Hebrew midwives Shiprah and Puah not wanting to kill the newborns. Here, creating a play that brings together several stories in an anachronistic setting by thematic issue gives an opportunity for your tweens to learn a broad number of stories and think through what connects them and how they connect to the life of your congregation and their lives as well.

Finally, writing a drama can also be a strategy for stories we know too well and are ready to learn again from a different perspective, such as the stories of Jesus' birth, stories of his death and resurrection, the creation stories in Genesis and their resonances in Job and Proverbs, over-taught parables (the Prodigal Son, the Sower, etc.). Familiarity can turn these stories into white noise in the background of tween lives. By stopping and focusing deeply on these familiar stories, young people can learn that these stories have staying power because of the multiple layers of meaning that are possible after sustained engagement with them.

DIGGING IN TO THE STORY

Once you have determined which story or set of stories is big enough for you to work with, it is time to dig into the story with your tweens. Since many of the stories can be long passages or even several chapters in the Bible, figuring out ways for your younger adolescents to work through them without turning this into something too much like school work is an important consideration. One of the ways that I help them get a sense of the big story, such as when I was trying to have them learn the whole story of Moses in order to figure out why he showed up in the transfiguration story, is to break up the longer narratives into sections that individuals or pairs of students read on behalf of the whole. Then I try to think of a fun way that they can teach their segment of the story to the whole group.

One way for them to report back is *storyboarding*, like a director does for a movie. Here they chose key moments to capture with images, and then they talk through their images for the rest of the class, retelling the story in the process. This can also be turning the story segment into a cartoon or a page in a graphic novel. One benefit of this process is that it creates a permanent artifact to hang around the room for the class to reconsider as they move forward with planning the drama, keeping what they felt were the major turning points of the story in front of them. I also have had them write something like episode summaries for the whole group, being as irreverent or sassy as they want in updating the dialogue or plot. Some of this dialogue or phrasing worked its way into our scripts over the years. Or, they can create a retelling from one of the lesser known characters or recasting the villain as the hero, a strategy they are often familiar with because of children's books that do this with classic Disney stories or the *Wicked* book series by Gregory Maguire based on L. Frank Baum's Oz novels.

These kinds of exploratory exercises can take an entire session just to work through the key moments in the story, but in the process tweens are already beginning to put the story into their own ideas or interpretations, discussing with a partner what is going

Part I: Learning the Method

on and what it means. They are beginning to create something of their own for a reason, in this case to bring their colleagues up to speed on the part of the story that they read. All of these activities are part of beginning to own the stories for themselves.

Another great exercise to engage with a biblical text is to read it out loud and very slowly, with the goal of generating as many questions about the text as possible (the good, the bad, and the silly). You can station two people at a whiteboard or large piece of paper to just catch the questions as they are called out. For example, the first sentence of the book of Jonah is: "Now the word of the Lord came to Jonah son of Amittai, saying, 'Go at once to Nineveh, that great city, and cry out against it; for their wickedness has come up before me" (1:1). Some of the questions generated by the tweens at my church from this sentence included:

- How did the word of the Lord come to Jonah?
- Why isn't there a messenger, a burning bush, or a sign mentioned by the author like in other Bible stories?
- Who is Amittai?
- Where is Nineveh?
- Why is Nineveh considered a great city?
- Why did they do to be considered so wicked?

With a little probing in commentaries and Bible dictionaries, even more questions come up for the youth:

- If Nineveh is the capital of the Assyrians, who are enemies of the Hebrews and their God, why does God bother sending a prophet to them?
- The name Jonah means dove. Why would this prophet be named that?

This can go on for a while. Such questions are exactly the kinds of questions good Bible scholars ask of the text. What you are teaching in this practice is the ability to actually see what is in the text rather than reading into the text what they know from their exposure to earlier interpretations. These interpretations, perhaps from *Veggie Tales* videos or children's Bible storybooks, often have predigested the moral of the story for them by foregrounding one particular interpretation of the meaning of the text.

Teaching tweens not to just skip over the details of the places and the names but instead to be curious about why they are present changes their stance towards the stories. By asking why and wondering about the story, they bring a posture of mystery, listening, and respect for the text rather than trying to tame or control it. Many of these questions will have no good answers, and that is good for young people to understand, too. It allows them to see the Bible as stranger as well as a friend, which pushes them to listen more carefully to the mystery of how the text speaks to us.[1] The exercise also encourages curiosity and questioning as a posture in relationship to the Bible rather than boredom or acceptance.

Such questioning can cause young people to explore what biblical scholars call intertextuality, that is, places in the Bible that link to and lift up other stories from other parts of the Bible. For instance, they might find out that "the word of the Lord" also shows up in Hosea 1:1; Joel 1:1; Micah 1;1, and other books about prophecy. This helps them understand that this is a stock literary form, not unlike "Once upon a time," that demonstrates that this prophetic character's inspiration and authority does not come from themselves but from God. So, the phrase doesn't necessarily indicate an actual event where the word of God came to Jonah in a particular form, but instead serves as a signal to listeners to pay attention to this guy.

For shorter stories it is easier to read the entire passage more quickly, but I still like to spend a while, even an entire session, just getting familiar with the story. Reading the story in multiple versions is one way to dig in and begin to notice subtle discrepancies between versions. For New Testament stories that occur in the Gospels, one good resource is a book of Gospel parallels that places any story that occurs in more than one of the four Gospels

---

1. O'Connor, "Crossing Borders," 329.

next to each other, which makes the changes in the story between Gospels much easier to see and analyze.[2]

For a shorter passage, reading what comes before and after the particular story you are working on allows the young people to ask why the story might occur at that particular point in the narrative. So, they may notice that the parable of the prodigal son comes immediately after parables about a lost coin and a lost sheep and ask why the author felt that all three needed to be told in a row. Or, the tweens may realize that the temptations in the wilderness happen just after Jesus' baptism and just before his public ministry starts and ask why that would happen to Jesus just at that moment in his life. Location matters in the story; the Gospels were crafted as written texts with a flow. Tweens are astute enough to see where it looks like a bad term paper, where an editor lumped things together because of thematic links but the flow is off, and where the sequencing seems to have a desired rhetorical effect.

Shorter stories can be explored by listening to the story being read out loud and trying to hear the events from the point of view of one particular character or group of people. Tweens can act out the story, and practice making different choices in how to say lines or enact situations that arise in the stories. They can retell the story in a new setting, or create an "in between the lines" document in which they write the thoughts that characters would be having but not saying aloud as the situation unfolds. All of these exercises help to hear what is actually in the text and to recognize what they are choosing to fill in from their own experience and imagination that may be missing in the text.

After engaging some of these exercises to begin to explore the story, I like to bring in commentaries and Bible dictionaries to help the young people answer as many of their own questions that have arisen through the exercises as possible. Many of these resources can be found in your pastor's office or in local libraries, if your church does not have them in its library. You can also check online resources, although be careful to find resources related to reliable sources, such as your denomination, universities, religious orders,

2. Throckmorton, *Gospel Parallels*.

or other sources. One skill that your youth will gain from having this kind of discernment performed in front of them is how to sort out what is found on the Internet about religion, as there is a lot of harmful misinformation out there.

Once the tweens have answered as many of the questions that they can, we revisit the questions we haven't been able to answer. Then we enjoy playing "ask the expert" with our pastor or another adult who has done a fair amount of Bible study in your congregation. This could be someone who has been through the Disciple Bible Study, Kerygma, Education for Ministry, or another intensive educational offering that includes reading large portions of the Bible. I happen to have colleagues on the seminary faculty and in my congregation with doctorates in biblical interpretation whom I have invited to come in and work with the young people at this point. What is amazing is how the questions that the youth can't find answers to are often the very same questions that experienced Bible scholars wrestle with or cannot answer. These experts or professionals are often amazed by how carefully the young people have examined the texts, and the sophistication of their ability to work with it when slowed down and taken seriously. Hearing that their work is affirmed by experts, whether the pastor, a trusted adult in the congregation, or a biblical scholar, really helps the young people feel competent with the text.

EXPLORING THE RECEPTION HISTORY

Any big-enough Bible story that you choose to engage with your young people has likely been the subject of poetry, visual art, hymns or songs, sermons, or literary references from some point in history. These artistic reflections of the biblical text are a part of what biblical scholars call the "reception history" of the text. They allow us to see what our ancestors in faith made of the stories we also struggle to understand. For tweens, these works of art give them a window into how other humans at other times have been inspired by the same story that they are engaging and have created something beautiful or disturbing based on the story, just as they themselves are about to do.

For example, bringing two distinctive visual works of art inspired by the story allows comparative work on what is engaging to different artists about the texts. Projecting the pieces on a wall and working with them individually lets your tweens answer questions like:

- What is going on in this picture?
- What catches your eye first? Where does use of light or color draw your attention?
- What elements of the story did the artist really seem drawn to?
- How did the artist portray the characters—strong, broken, a leader? What are their relationships? What emotions are they expressing?
- What is different from what is happening in this picture to the picture in your head when you read the story? (This is a beginning interpretive question about perspective and how prior experience or knowledge affects how we hear the text).

A second art piece can be worked through with similar questions. After working through the next artist, you can put up both pieces of art side by side and again ask what is different about the way the two authors portrayed the story, and how that differs from their own conversation about it. This is a great opportunity to begin to talk about how we interpret stories, using our own experiences, values, and notions of what is beautiful to make sense of the story. Together you can explore how what is important to different people in different times and locations from the stories is valid and interesting.

Many biblical stories have inspired poems and songs as well as visual art, and their texts and music can also be explored with tweens. Again, you can explore differences in interpretations of the story by reading aloud and/or listening to one or more examples and exploring questions such as:

- What part of the story does this song/poem focus on most intensely?
- What emotions does the poet give the characters?
- What seems to be motivating the character in the poem?
- What is the important idea that the poet wants to say in the poem?
- Is that what we thought was important about the story? Why might they be interested in this other piece of the story?

One of the gifts of Internet search engines and the sheer amount of data they can generate for you is that finding these kinds of artifacts inspired by the text (art work, songs, poems, sermons) is easier than ever. In a smaller class, these can be explored without a projector on a computer, phone, or a tablet screen that is passed around.

EMBRACING THE UNORTHODOX

As you will discover as you pull up a variety of art pieces and songs related to biblical stories, artistic reflections give the freedom and the permission for artists to bring themselves to the biblical text, to engage their own questions and wonderings about the stories, and to embed them in their own time and context far from the original. Asking your tweens to create their own drama related to the story invites them to bring themselves to the story as an equal to earlier artists. By encouraging the intellectual engagement with the story through asking questions and seeking answers in commentaries and other resources, you communicate that such work is faithful and not a free-for-all projection onto the text, but a disciplined interpretive engagement. However, the resulting connections and insights they make may not replicate the "correct" theology embraced by your community. One question leaders need to consider prior to beginning the process is how to respond to this lack of orthodoxy in a way that encourages rather than shuts down biblical study and interpretation.

Part I: Learning the Method

One of the surprises in working with tweens is how two motivating factors tend to dominate their connections with the biblical text: the absurd and the funny. Trying to be funny was perhaps the primary motivation for the kids with whom I have worked. They were also truly absurd sometimes, and sometimes the absurdity worked its way into our plays. For example, in the post-resurrection encounters with Jesus, my tweens were intrigued by why the disciples seemed to suddenly understand things when Jesus spoke to them or merely appeared to them, even though what Jesus actually said didn't seem to grant the same understanding to contemporary readers of the story. One kid jokingly said it was like Jesus performed a Jedi mind trick on them, which became a running inside joke about Jesus. In response to the running joke, I had a couple of options. One was to take a stance that Jesus' teaching was not deceptive or forceful like a Jedi mind trick, and they should stop thinking about it that way. Another was to join them in this metaphor and see what it did to our story. Unorthodox? Absolutely. Creating connections and love for the story and the bumbling disciples trying to figure out their own legacy left by their dead and resurrected messiah? Also true. Fortunately, I am in a congregation where the adults have a pretty high tolerance for treating the biblical stories irreverently. Maybe this is a skill you will have to coach in your own congregation.

Obviously, I come down on the side of allowing freedom of interpretation, even when it tends towards the absurd. If your community cannot tolerate this kind of theological and spiritual freedom in making connections, working with the adults ahead of time to strategize how to respond to interpretations or ideas that do not fit the community's standards of interpretation is doubly important. Inviting tweens into using their minds and imaginations to engage the text but then telling them that their engagement is inadequate or not permissible will likely cause frustration and rebellion if not handled with grace and aplomb. Be sure that adults do not just shut down the conversation, but instead positively express the values that the members of the congregation hold that might be violated by the interpretation. Then they can help tweens try to work within that value to say what they are hoping to say in order to encourage development for the tween's interpretive power within the norms of the community.

Something else that caused both amusement and annoyance in my tweens was the apparent unfairness in the biblical text of leaving out the names of some characters that seem central to a story. The tweens always relished getting to fill in the missing monikers with the most ridiculous contemporary names they could think of. This is how the second disciple on the road to Emmaus has been forever immortalized in our minds as Howard. Or, how the three Marys who witnessed the resurrection in various accounts caused the kids to have a terrible time keeping them apart in their own minds. Some of the tweens were also a little annoyed that they all had the same name and were identified primarily by whose mother they were, which changes from one Gospel to another. So this became a visual joke in the play by having the characters wearing t-shirts with "Mary, mother of Jesus" and "Mary, mother of somebody" on the front, as well as a strong rewriting of their contributions to the early church continuing after Jesus' death. Perhaps this was not the most respectful or historically accurate treatment of the first proclaimers of the resurrection, but they were honest expressions of an older elementary school sense of justice that the women should be more clearly and consistently remembered in the sacred text. Here they join the witness of second-wave feminist scholars, who also spent a great deal of time trying to recover the history and dignity of women whose stories the biblical text doesn't always record. The tweens did not know that history, but they did have expectations for gender equality in their own setting that worked its way into the script.

These inside jokes about "Jesus as Jedi" or "Mary, mother of somebody" made the stories their stories: theirs to play with, theirs to listen to, theirs to argue with, theirs to be in relationship with. But they also helped to create a group of tweens with a shared story and an experience with it of which only they knew the full origins. These kinds of connections are at the heart of writing the play, a process to which we now turn.

5

Creating and Producing the Play

AFTER FOUR OR MORE weeks of engaging with the story on a weekly basis, working through their questions about it, entering into it imaginatively, and seeing what other artists, poets, and songwriters have done with it, tweens can turn their minds towards creating the play they will share with the congregation. Many times ideas will have cropped up in the exploration of the text, so the first step might be to simply track those as they emerge and write them down. In particular, the experiences and connections they have made with their own lives are important to consider here. What part of the stories did they find most engaging to their own minds and hearts? What elements of the story sparked curiosity and ignited conversation, even digressions or seemingly random connections? What was weird or interesting to them? What little inside jokes built a kind of camaraderie around the stories that would not have been there had we been treating them with appropriate reverence? These are the places that are alive in the text in relation to the tweens' lives, and the most important places to work with in beginning the creation of the play.

CREATING AND PRODUCING THE PLAY

WHAT DOES IT SAY TO THE COMMUNITY?

The connections that the tweens make with the story are perhaps the easiest to note and keep track of. The next step is a bigger challenge for younger adolescents, as it calls for the kind of empathy for others that is only an emerging skill in this age group. Being asked to discern what will connect to the broader church audience for which they will be performing is a real stretch for tweens, requiring that they imagine how the adults in the congregation will experience their interpretations. Fortunately, this is where the intergenerational community comes into play. There will be at least one and hopefully several adults working with the young people. They can help the young people begin to identify what in the story might speak to the experiences of the larger congregation.

One thing that tweens do pay attention to are the hurts, joys, and other emotional extremes of the congregation. So, it may help to begin to ask, "What is going on with the people in our congregation right now?" They hopefully can hear about some of these life issues in prayer time in worship, or perhaps you can bring a bulletin, newsletter, or emails that ask for prayer and support for new parents, or for those struggling with illness and grief, for the young people to encounter. They can share what they know is going on in their families and in the circles to which they are connected, and the adults can share what they know is going on, or add the perspective of longer experience to what the tweens are seeing. This is not meant to be a gossip fest about the lives of congregants, but an honest assessment of what is hard for people in hearing local, national, and global news, in navigating everyday life, and where this connects with the struggles of the characters in the play.

For example, not many of us have experienced giving up everything to follow a leader who then is brutally executed by an occupying empire like the disciples in these-post resurrection stories. But many people have believed in something or someone only to discover later that they weren't all that they had expected and have felt the disillusionment and disorientation of that discovery. This is a hard connection for young people to make on behalf of

Part I: Learning the Method

the adults in the congregation, but it is a connection they can make with a little adult help. As an added benefit, practicing imagining the perspective of the congregation in seeing and hearing their play builds adolescents' skills for empathy and intergenerational connection. Although difficult for participants, this is an important growing edge in their social and emotional development, as well as their capacity to love their neighbors.

FINDING A FRAME

After thinking about what connections are essential to the tweens and their elders in the congregation, we begin to try to find a frame or setting for our play. I always feel a little desperate until we figure out what we will be the frame for our play, because the process of creation does not feel like it will happen until this idea comes into focus. By "frame" I mean the conceit that allows the characters to speak in a dramatic format that works for the constraints that our environment presents.

Sometimes we have written dramas that are literally an enactment of the story. We have performed skits about the Bible characters without any framing device or narrators, simply trying to represent our version of the story. More often we have an out-of-context contemporary framing: a newscast about a biblical event, a green room on a talk show, or a snarky commentator on the events as they unfold. These frames generally come about because they allow the tweens to insert their personal observations and wonderment into the narrative while marking a separation between the world within the Bible story and the world they are living in as they read it and try to understand it. These devices have always come from the tweens in my experience, often as we are exploring the connections that they have made that they want to share with the congregation. The moment of figuring out the frame of the play always seems to take some creative mystery and inspiration, but it has almost always come from the young people in my class.

As we are making connections to the story and exploring the reception history through art and poetry, the participants often begin to brainstorm "what if we" or "maybe we could" suggestions for the structure of the play, and eventually energy coalesces around one of the ideas. Often the initial brainstorming is unrealistically grand and would require more resources, strategies, or special effects than we can muster. Others are hopelessly silly. Your goal is to listen and to figure out what is possible within their wild imaginings. This is a moment of trust in the Holy Spirit for inspiration, and sometimes it can take a while, but waiting on the presence of the Holy Spirit in interpretation is a spiritual skill for tweens to learn as well.

The next step is to begin to ask which characters in the story or roles in the play the tweens best fit. This always feels like a slightly magical moment in the creation of the play for me. In my years of writing plays with tweens we never held auditions or had an adult make decisions about how to cast the play, where we were forced to choose between candidates who both want the same role. Somehow, the group always sorted itself into the roles for the play. At some point as we were beginning to establish the frame for the play, someone would be dying to play a certain character and would beg to do so. This would inevitably lead to a conversation where other people also claimed their preferences and favorite roles. We always have some young people who are hesitant to take on any role at all. We sometimes have created characters or non-speaking roles for those who didn't want to speak in public. But we have always chosen roles before we wrote the play, so that the play could be written to the strengths and reservations of the participants in the class.

WRITING THE PLAY

Here's a little secret. In the end, I wrote the first draft of all of the plays. I have experimented over the years with letting the tweens write the plays, but that has never worked. I think that asking them to write the plays feels too much like homework, and they lose the sense of joy in it. We would lose momentum waiting for them to get done, and they would feel overburdened by the process. Unless

Part I: Learning the Method

you have a young person in your community who has a particular gift for creative writing, this is probably not a task that one of your tweens will do without a lot of support. So, over the years I have decided that I am going to harvest as many jokes, ideas, dialogue, framing devices, and connections from the youth that I can, and then craft them into the play on my own at home. This generally only takes a couple of hours for me, but is a heavier burden than any one of the tweens wants to take on by themselves. Writing it all in the same room by committee is nearly impossible. So having an adult do the first draft seems to work best.

The balance in writing is to try to make it into something coherent, while also mostly using the ideas that the youth have come up with on their own. When we have the table read the next week, I want to be sure that they feel like there is nothing in the play that they don't recognize, understand, or like. There have been a few times where I have had to add a few things on my own for coherence or theological connection that I had to then explain to the participants, but generally after several weeks of working with the stories, there is plenty to work with, and the hard part is trying to stuff in all of the good ideas while keeping it within the time bounds available.

I draft the play, and the next week we have a table read. During the table read, the tweens know that they have editorial control over dialogue and other content. I always tell them that I want the words to feel right in their mouths. They have certainly improved the dialogue over the years, and clarified some of my worst moments of theological jargon. I have the linguistic disadvantage of having a doctorate in theology, and that often makes me talk in ways that aren't the clearest to fourth- through eighth-graders. The tweens are great at finding those spots and helping make them flow better and be more understandable to the whole congregation.

The table read is always such an exciting day! The tweens can see their work coming to fruition in the play. They feel affirmed because their jokes, their ideas, their themes and connections are worked into it, and now it is something that really exists that they are going to perform! We also use that read through to begin to imagine what props, costumes, and staging would work for this particular play.

BUT I'M NOT A THEATER PERSON!

I am right with you. I too have very little background in theater production. So, even though I have been using the terms "drama" or "play," in reality what we have performed are perhaps better characterized as skits or dramatic narrative sermons. Whatever keeps your expectations low for production values, go with that image.

Basically, we have had to make due with one table read in the Sunday school classroom, one extended (two-hour) rehearsal where we deal with blocking, sound, and prop issues, and one final dress rehearsal on the Sunday morning we are going to perform. That's it. Perhaps if you have lots of theater experience, a worship space that allows for sets or lighting, and youth able to get to the church outside of Sunday morning, you could engage in a more elaborate production with extended rehearsals, full memorization of lines, and coaching about the acting. We never had those resources, so part of our creativity was keeping it simple and within the limits of our technological bounds and theatrical skill level.

Only a few things are essential for the congregation. The play must feel authentic to the young people who create it, and the congregation must be able to hear and follow along. For example, you will notice that in most of these sample plays we tend to have two narrator-types and two main characters or groupings of characters who are speaking at any given time. Basically, this format emerged because our worship space has two side lecterns/pulpits with affixed microphones that are permanently linked into the sound system, one lavalier microphone, and one handheld microphone. So, after one disastrous play in which half of the congregation could not hear anything the kids said, this configuration of microphones has always impacted how we design our plays. Nothing makes the adults in our congregations more frustrated and antsy than feeling

Part I: Learning the Method

like the kids are leading worship and they can't hear a word they are saying.

Additionally, we have always worked with a minimal/nonexistent budget, so we have had to work with either the Christmas pageant costumes that our church owned already, iron-on t-shirts as our primary costuming device, or with the clothes the tweens already own. Sometimes we have even made jokes in the plays about how we always have the same costumes, such as having narrators confuse a character with the last one who wore the same costume. But maybe you have an adult or young person in your community who is inspired by *Project Runway* and wants to serve as your costumer. Maybe you want to make your play a musical because you have a great minister of music who is excited about the event. Great! You can play to the strengths of your community and invest where you have the resources, and make do creatively where they are not present. Make it your own and have fun with it. My experience has been that the congregation is happy to see the young people investing in the stories of the Christian tradition, and they will play along with a wide range of skill levels and performance qualities.

Part II

Sample Dramas

In this section you will find several of the dramas that I have written with a couple of generational cycles of tweens in my own congregation. They are here for you to get a sense of what a drama written by younger adolescents would look like, and to get a feel for the way we are taking the Bible both seriously and playfully in our work with it as we create our own plays.

You are welcome to use these plays in your own congregation. While I would ask that you give credit to the authors (Katherine Turpin and the Youth of Christ Church United Methodist in Denver, Colorado), you are welcome to use them to your own ends. If you feel intimidated by writing your own play, you could use a modified process of getting to know the texts involved and then use these plays as part of your reception history. The young people will become familiar with the biblical stories by performing the plays, so this is a viable approach to learning the texts. They will, however, miss out on the joyful act of creation and of seeing their ideas and interpretations coming to life in front of the congregation.

You could also use these as a jumping off place to create your own play, inviting the tweens in your congregation to spring off of these stories and improve them with their own knowledge of the text. However, they will probably be most helpful to you as an inspiration and reality check about the wonderful dramas that could be created by your own adolescents.

As someone who may be considering this method in your own church, in reading through the plays you can see the way their connections emerged and played out with the stories a bit more concretely. Behind the plays for me are the young people who wrestled, created, and grew into faithful young adults while writing them, as well as the visitors who dropped in for a few months, shared this experience with us, and moved on to other communities and locales. Based on the groupings of the youth we had in the community in any given year, sometimes these were written by fourth- through eighth-graders, sometimes middle- and high-schoolers worked together, and many combinations in between.

6

In the Green Room
A Post-Pageant Christmas Reflection

INTRODUCTION

EVERY YEAR OUR CONGREGATION has an impromptu, unrehearsed Christmas pageant during a Sunday morning service of lessons and carols held during Advent. (I know; you can call a liturgical foul for reading the Christmas story and singing Christmas songs during Advent.) Because the older elementary and middle school youth were beginning to feel too old to put on the shepherd and wise person costumes and resisted participation in the pageant, we decided one year to write a play together to be used as the proclamation of the word in response to the Christmas pageant readings and carols.

In preparation to write the play, we read carefully through the birth narratives in the first and second chapters of Luke and Matthew. One of the activities we engaged was writing down the names of all of the characters who appeared in these stories who weren't usually in the Christmas pageant, didn't show up in the nativity scenes, and were not culturally associated with Christmas

Part II: Sample Dramas

for the tweens. We then figured out who they were and asked two simple questions: Why did the Gospel writers think these people were important enough to include? And why doesn't the church tell their stories when it celebrates Christmas today? The resulting conversations led to the creation of this play.

A green room is the place where persons about to go onstage in a live television show wait their turn. In this play, biblical characters from the birth narratives in the Gospels of Luke and Matthew who do not normally appear in Christmas pageants sit together backstage in the green room and talk about why they don't get to play a major role onstage. In the meantime, they help us all remember that God works through ordinary people to achieve extraordinary ends, which is the point of connection that the young people imagined was worth sharing with the congregation. This play was originally performed by six tweens and two adult mentors.

If you knew the young people who wrote and performed the play, you would understand why Gabriel is a goth, why the Holy Spirit comes across as kind of cranky, and why Elizabeth is assertive, if not a little aggressive. Those are the personalities of the young people who shaped the role and voice of the characters. You know how television writers talk about writing for their actors? That happened here as well, and the congregation who knew those young people loved the personal touch.

SCRIPTURE PASSAGES

Matthew 1–2 and Luke 1:18—2:23

CHARACTERS

Narrator/Holy Spirit
Elizabeth
Zechariah
Anna

Simeon
Gabriel
Herod
Herod's Assistant

STAGING

We used a few armchairs that were set up in the front of the sanctuary where the pageant had just taken place. Other than simple costuming (largely leftovers from the robes and angel wings from our usual pageant costumes), black cardboard wings, and a flaming sword for Gabriel, and coffee mugs from the church kitchen, no other props were used. High-tech trumpet sound effects were provided by a smartphone held up to the microphone, but it could have been a trumpet player from middle school band if one had been handy.

SCRIPT

Narrator: (*offstage into microphone*) Meanwhile, back in the Green Room . . .

Elizabeth, Zechariah, Anna, and Simeon lounge about on their chairs, drinking out of coffee mugs.

Simeon: I can't believe it. Another Christmas pageant has come and gone, and here we are, still waiting offstage to play our parts.

Zechariah: I know it. Some years even that dratted innkeeper gets a speaking part, and he doesn't even show up in the Bible! I could be really entertaining. After all, I spent nine months struck totally silent just because I didn't believe that messenger during the offering of incense. Think of the dramatic possibilities!

Simeon begins to mime dramatically, waving arms about and mouthing words.

Anna: Tell me about it. I might as well have been one of the unnamed women in the Bible if no one bothers to read my story

Part II: Sample Dramas

in church once in a while. I mean, it's not like they have a lot of women prophets to choose from. Sure, male prophets are a dime a dozen in the Hebrew Bible. But there's only a few of us women prophets who are remembered. Anna—that's me—Deborah, and poor Huldah—such an unfortunate name.

Elizabeth: (*interrupting*) Well, how about me? After all that Zechariah and I went through, you'd think that maybe someone would keep *my* part of the story in their pageant, but nope. They always skip over the beginning and jump right to Bethlehem. Let me tell you, it was a long nine months for Mary, and what would she have done if she didn't have our home to come hide out in? All of those tongues wagging and Joseph thinking about leaving the poor child. Nobody seems to remember Zechariah and me and all we endured. The rumors, (*emphatically, pointing at Zechariah*) nine months of that one waving about and mouthing (*imitates him unkindly*).

Simeon: Now, now, we all know that it was a tough time for you both. But, after all of those years of waiting, wasn't it great to be given the gift of your own son, and didn't that John turn out to be something? I mean, people thought he was Elijah, for heaven's sake! He got to baptize the Messiah! Wasn't that worth it?

Zechariah: Sure, but don't you think people would benefit from hearing our stories, too? The little kids dressed as animals are cute, and everybody likes an angel with a crooked tinsel halo and coat hanger wings, but we were where all of the action was happening. Real people faced with real challenges, having really wild encounters with God, and the courage to carry out this crazy plan, and nobody seems to remember us.

Gabriel enters from the side, fast, dramatic, and strong with a trumpet blast. He is dressed in a goth angel costume with crazy wings and makeup. Everybody jumps in fright, then cowers under their chairs.

Gabriel: What? What? (*looking around*) Oh, right, be not afraid.

Gabriel crosses the front of the stage and stands with arms crossed looking regally around the sanctuary. Other characters begin to climb back up into their seats as the Holy Spirit floats and flutters in, spinning gently.

Holy Spirit: Must you always make such an entrance, Gabriel? It always puts people in such a state. (*She wanders around, comforting other characters, patting their backs and cupping their cheeks gently, speaking in a wispy voice.*) There, there, you will be just fine. Where two or three are gathered, I will be there also. I blow where I will, bringing my fruits of joy and patience and whatnot. Spirit, wind, breath, *ruach*. (*ends with a curtsy*)

Anna: So, you two got left out again this year, too?

Holy Spirit: (*sighs*) Yes, they always start out by invoking me, but then never actually tell what part I had in the whole story. You think it's easy making a baby in such an (*pauses, looks at the congregation and clears throat*) unusual way without completely freaking out the mother? But, I'm used to my work going largely unnoticed. The Father (*points to sky*), the Son (*points to cross*), they get all the attention. But I'm the one who really gets things done: moving through the hearts of people, helping them be inspired to live as God's children. Since I'm subtle (*looks pointedly at Gabriel*), I'm often overlooked. I'm used to it. (*shrugs amiably*)

Elizabeth: No disrespect, Gabriel, but what is up with that outfit?

Gabriel: Well, I just needed something to make me, well, stand out a little bit.

Elizabeth: (*looking for a fight*) The ability to drop in on people, announce completely startling news, then condemn them to silence for months on end not enough power for ya?

Zechariah: (*pulls Elizabeth back*) It was a long time ago, dear.

Gabriel: Well, people can never remember that I'm Gabriel, the Angel of the Lord. Some people even want to call me Michael, for heaven's sake. Darn it, if I have to do God's messenger boy dirty work, I want people to know who I am. The name is Gabriel, Angel of the Lord. (*trumpet sounds again*)

Part II: Sample Dramas

Simeon: Greetings, favored one (*a little sarcastically*). So, you didn't make the cut either?

Gabriel: Well, I did put in a cameo as a part of the whole heavenly host, but I don't think anybody even recognized me. (*sits dejectedly in a chair*)

Simeon: Why do you think people don't want to remember us in that story? I guess they kind of have to keep in Mary and Joseph, but why focus on a bunch of drunken shepherds in the field and wise men from afar? Why don't they want to remember the regular folk at the center of this all? People like me and Anna, who lived in the temple day in and day out, faithfully waiting to see the fulfillment of God's promise?

Zechariah: Or people like me and Elizabeth, living out the traditions of our ancestors, faithful to God despite the disappointment of never being blessed with children?

Anna: Are they scared to believe that a normal woman can be called to be a prophetess of God?

Elizabeth: Maybe they are scared that God will call them to play a part, too? Don't want any freaky angels showing up in their dreams.

Holy Spirit: (*dreamily*) I don't know. I think it has to do with which parts got put into the nativity scenes. Those funny humans really like their little manger scenes. (*touching the one on the altar*) I'm kind of hard to capture in wood and plaster.

Herod and his personal assistant enter from the door behind the pulpit. Herod walks as a king, slow and regal. His assistant dithers and shuffles parchment.

Gabriel: (*steps up to stop him, raising his flaming sword*) You have no business here, Herod.

found him, bring me word so that I may also go and pay him homage.'" And later on he helps Jesus fulfill the prophecies about Egypt and Nazareth. So you see, given the signs and warrants provided by the Holy Scriptures, Herod is by right a significant part of the Christmas story as recorded in the Gospel of Matthew, and accorded all of the rights and responsibilities there unto, as noted by the chief priests and scribes of the people.

Herod: What she said.

Holy Spirit: (*joining Gabriel, and looking a little fierce*) It seems to me that she conveniently left out the part about you slaughtering all of those babies and toddlers in Bethlehem, and later your own wife and children, to maintain your power. Every time I try, I find your heart is a stone that cannot be penetrated, Herod. You have no business here.

Herod: Oh come on, every story needs a villain. These Christmas pageants would be a lot more interesting if they didn't write me out of them. Back in the Middle Ages I was the star of the show. One of the most famous morality plays was called . . . wait for it . . . "Herod" (*makes a hand motion as if it is written on a marquee*). Now, everyone's afraid that they will scare the children, so it's all sweetness and light, bathrobes and fuzzy sheep. Where's the fear? Where's the dramatic tension, I ask you? Where's the reality?

Gabriel: You had your moment. You took every opportunity possible to take care of yourself and keep your power, caring nothing about those you hurt along the way. We have no need to remember that. We have plenty of examples of that every day. Leave now!

Part II: Sample Dramas

Anna: Is he gone?

Zechariah: Whew! That is one evil dude.

Simeon: He kind of has a point, though.

All except Holy Spirit: What!?!

Simeon: Well, he is a part of the story. If Matthew thought he was important to keep in, don't you think we might have something to learn from him?

All pause, considering and looking at one another.

All except Holy Spirit: Nah. Nope. Uh-uh, etc.

Elizabeth: They say the Lord works in mysterious ways, and goodness knows I've seen enough to believe it. But I can't think of one way that that (*starts a few choice names, sputters and looks at Holy Spirit*) man could be used by God.

Holy Spirit: You'd be surprised who God can use (*points to the figures on the altar*). An unwed teenage mother, a bunch of drunken shepherds, prostitutes and tax collectors, (*indicates Gabriel with head*) a stuck-up angel, (*looks at Elizabeth and Zechariah*) a dried up priest and his ancient wife, an old church mouse of a prophetess, a righteous man (*smiles at Simeon*)—all can be used by God, if they keep their hearts and minds open and listen. That's what all of you did, so many years ago.

Anna: So why don't they remember us?

Zechariah: Yeah, why don't they tell our stories?

Simeon: Well, it is a bit scary to have Gabriel showing up and telling you crazy things will happen.

Elizabeth: And it is the holiday season, some kind of feast day, I think. Remember when we celebrated the Festival of Booths that year, and John tried to climb up on top of ours, Zechariah?

Zechariah: (*laughs*) I could have killed him. What a mess. Well, Anna, Simeon, better luck next year, I guess. Peace be with you.

Elizabeth and Zechariah exit together.

Simeon: And with you, friends. Same time, same place next year?

Anna: (*looking out over congregation*) One of these years, one of those little girls in the pageant is gonna graduate from angel to (*with emphasis and pointing to her chest*) prophetess.

Gabriel: Hey!

Anna: Truth to power, girls! Come on, Mr. Simeon the Righteous, I know where we can get some better coffee.

Simeon: You know, I think righteousness is underrated. People hear the word and think self-righteousness, but they are two totally different things. Maybe I should change from Simeon the Righteous to Simeon Who Was Totally Down with God. What do you think?

Gabriel: It has potential. See you around?

Anna: (*comically startled*) Why?

Simeon: (*also quaking*) Does God have plans for us?

Gabriel: (*sighs*) Be not afraid. (*Anna and Simeon relax a bit.*) None that I'm aware of. Peace be with you.

Anna and Simeon: And with you.

Simeon: Spirit, come with us?

Holy Spirit: I always do. (*curtsies to Gabriel, then glides away*)

Gabriel: (*waits until they leave, then looks out over congregation, pointing at them*) Don't forget, that's Gabriel, Angel of the Lord. Coming to a dream near you. Be afraid; be very afraid.

Holy Spirit: (*offstage*) Gabriel! They are hard enough to work with already.

Gabriel: Oh all right. (*more formally*) Do not be afraid, for you have found favor with God. (*walks away muttering*) I guess nothing is impossible with God.

7

MST 3000
The Transfiguration

INTRODUCTION

I WANT TO SAY something about the parody that emerged in our work with the story of the Transfiguration. On the one hand, the tweens made the link to a bad science fiction movie as they read the story over and over again, and that is where the connection to *Mystery Science Theater* emerged. Our use of this idea was largely a sign of desperation. The tweens were trying to make the congregation laugh more than I was willing to work into the actual script. But as I thought about it, the format fits a bit. When we watch the transfiguration story play out, it is a little bit like a weird sci-fi flick. What does it mean that Jesus lit up and glowed? And these other figures from another time showing up? It is an experience that may call for a little distance rather than moving right into it. Plus, they had been overinfluenced by snark. No doubt. But we worked with it.

In the play you can see how they made connections to their own cultural touchstones. For example, the only context they had for the word "transfiguration" was Professor McGonagall's class in the Harry Potter books, so she gets a shout-out. So does the song about Rudolph the Red-Nosed Reindeer. Their weird fascination with the story about Elijah and the bears from their prep work make an appearance, too. In all of these little connections you can see the work they did with trying to understand the story in its literary and historical context.

Some of the more subtle life-resonance connections you may notice as you read are the way that Moses and Elijah sound a little bit like unwise middle school friends egging on Jesus towards violent misbehavior. I'm guessing in not many other places does the transfiguration show up as a story connected to peer pressure in middle school, but my tweens made that connection in the way the story was reconstructed. You can also see that our congregation was fighting for marriage equality in Colorado at the time that this play was written, so some references to that get written into the play.

You can also see us struggling with the limitations of our abilities to make special effects happen in our very bright Sunday morning sanctuary (and our lack of budget for a fog machine). They decided to make fun of our own terrible special effects once they got over the frustration of not being able to make their various creative visions come to life as they imagined a much grander play. We also had gender-blind casting, as this story has all male characters. Therefore, Elijah, Jesus, James, and Peter were all played by tween girls in this one.

SCRIPTURE PASSAGES

Mark 9:1-8; Matthew 17:1-13; Luke 9:28-36; 1 Kings 17-19; Exodus 1-24

CHARACTERS

Narrator 1

Part II: Sample Dramas

Narrator 2
Jesus
Peter
James
John
Elijah
Moses

SCRIPT

Narrator 1: Good morning. Before we begin this morning's sermon, we want to explain the genre of our play. *Mystery Science Theater 3000* is a cable show that shows truly bad science fiction movies produced decades ago, like *Hercules and the Moon Men*.

Narrator 2: The premise of the show is that three characters are trapped by a villain and forced to watch these cheesy movies. So, while the movies are running, the characters sit in front of the screen and make snarky comments about the movie. We have chosen to present our transfiguration play in this same format so we could incorporate our sense of humor into our message.

Narrator 1: We hope you enjoy the show.

Jesus, Peter, James, and John walk down the main aisle of the sanctuary, acting as if they are trudging up a mountain. Jesus seems very perky, the other three disciples less so.

James: Where are we going?

Jesus: (*points*) Up to the top of this mountain to pray.

Peter and John: Again?

Narrator 1: Oooh, it's like Bible Outward Bound!

Narrator 2: Hope the bears don't come out and maul them.

Narrator 1: Wrong story.

Peter: Why do we always have to climb the mountain to pray? Can't we pray just as well on flat land?

Jesus: So all of those people we just taught will leave us alone. (*They walk a minute.*)

James: Isn't this the same mountain Elijah climbed when he was running away from that queen?

John: Isabelle? Or Anabelle?

Narrator 1: Lulubelle?

Narrator 2: (*singing*) Ring, ring, ring went the trolley. Ding, ding, ding went the bell.

Jesus: (*frowns at narrators*) It was Queen *Jezebel*. That was no joke. Elijah was running for his life. Fortunately nobody wants to kills us right this minute.

John: What do you mean, "right this minute"?

Peter: Yes, I wanted to talk to you about that. What was all of that about the Son of Man having to die and rise again?

James: You are not supposed to die. You are supposed to lead us all triumphant-like into Jerusalem.

John: Yeah, and stick it to those Romans!

Peter: You shouldn't say stuff like that about dying. It makes people nervous.

James: It makes *me* nervous.

Narrator 2: He shouldn't wear stuff like that either. Wasn't Joseph wearing that same robe in that awful Christmas movie?

Narrator 1: The one where the cow kept wandering off screen?

Narrator 2: Yeah, and they had that really tall guy in a fat suit playing Herod?

Narrator 1: (*snickers*) And some of them were reading their lines?

James: You can heal people.

John: And crowds of people show up to listen every time you preach!

Peter: God needs you. You're not gonna die.

Part II: Sample Dramas

Jesus: I'm not so sure how this is going to work out. For now, I need to clear my head and pray for a bit.

James: I'm pretty tired. All right if we just stay here and rest?

John: Yeah, I could nap.

Narrator 1: This play is putting me to sleep, too.

Jesus: Can you just stay awake and pray with me? I think I'm going to need the support.

Disciples: All right. Whatever (*or similar agreement*).

Jesus walks across the stage to the other side. The disciples yawn and stretch and settle like they are about to fall asleep. As Jesus gets all set to pray, suddenly Moses and Elijah pop out from off stage.

John: Whoa, who is that?

Narrator 2: Looks like ZZ Top.

Narrator 1: That one dude looks like a squirrel died on his face.

Narrator 2: Did they even have a budget for costumes?

James: Wait, is that Elijah? I thought John the Baptist was supposed to be Elijah! I never get what's happening around here.

Peter: It is Elijah . . . and Moses. The law and the prophets, right there with Jesus. Oh my God!

John: Look, his clothes are dazzling white!

Jesus rips off his outer robe to reveal a white one underneath.

Narrator 1: Instant laundry.

Narrator 2: Better than OxiClean.

James: And his face is glowing like Moses' did.

John: When he came down from the mountain after meeting God!

Narrator 1 and 2: (*sing*) Like a light bulb.

Narrator 1: They won't need a flashlight to get back down the mountain.

Narrator 2: They can just follow Jesus' head!

Peter: He's been transfigured!

Narrator 1: What is this, McGonagall's class from Harry Potter?

The disciples begin falling to the ground in fear and trembling. An adult walks by with a big posterboard cloud marked "cloud."

Narrator 1: These special effects are terrible.

Narrator 2: It's like this play was produced in 33 A.D. or something.

Voice of God from offstage: (*deep*) This is my son, in whom I am well pleased. Listen to him.

Narrator 1: Even God sounds a little like Darth Vader.

Jesus: Moses, Elijah.

Moses: Good to see you, man.

Elijah: Glad we could make it.

Moses: I see the followers haven't gotten much better since I was the prophet.

Jesus: They're not so bad.

Elijah: Could've fooled me. They were sleeping earlier.

Jesus: Yes, this has all been a bit hard for them to understand. Makes them a little whiny.

Moses: Boy, do I know what you mean. (*in whining voice*) "We're tired." "We're hungry." "We wanna go back to Egypt."

Elijah: (*sarcastically*) Who, us? We didn't help kill those prophets. No, no, Elijah did that all by himself. Totally innocent here.

Moses: I wish God had made "No whining" one of the Ten Commandments. Would've made my life easier.

Jesus: (*laughs*) That's pretty good. "Thou shalt not murder. Thou shalt not commit adultery. Thou shalt not whine."

Peter: What's that he said? No more wine?

James: But I like wine!

Narrator 1: Especially when it's a nice cabernet.

Part II: Sample Dramas

Narrator 2: And served with some tasty cheese and those little wheat crackers.

John: That can't be what he said. Jesus likes wine.

James: I distinctly heard it. "Thou shall not drink wine."

Peter: That's gonna make our after-supper story time a lot less interesting.

Moses: So, it looks like things are going to get kind of bad for you.

Jesus: Looks like.

Elijah: Why is it that we prophets always have to go up against the big guys?

Moses: Like Pharoah.

Elijah: King Ahaz. And (*shudders visibly*) Jezebel.

Jesus: I wouldn't have wanted to cross her. She meant business.

Moses: Those scribes and Pharisees aren't much easier to deal with. People get all bent out of shape when they are defending their religion.

Elijah: Yeah, what is that? "Don't touch that, it's unclean!" "Don't eat that, it's impure!" "Don't love him, that's an abomination!" Sheesh.

Jesus: They do tend to totally miss the point, don't they? So, you guys have a lot of experience. How do you think I should play this?

Elijah: This healing and teaching isn't going to get it for you. You're gonna have to pull out the big stuff. Rain fire down from the sky like me. Kill off all the opposition.

Moses: Yeah. Plagues. Nile into blood. Parting the Red Sea. That stuff really gets them to toe the line.

Narrator 1: Yeah, you gotta go all Chuck Norris on them, Jesus!

Narrator 2: My way or the highway.

Jesus: Killing off a bunch of people isn't exactly my style. (*shakes head sadly*) All those Egyptians dead in the sea. You know, Moses, they weren't so bad. They sheltered my family when Herod was trying to have me killed.

Elijah: Are you saying I shouldn't have killed those prophets? Sometimes it's them or you, Jesus.

Jesus: (*quietly*) Yeah, that's what I'm beginning to think, too. I was just hoping that if I became one of them, they could see me like a normal person.

Moses: Normal people don't change water into wine.

Elijah: (*pointedly at Moses*) Or rivers into blood. Ick.

Jesus: I know. I figured out after that wedding that they would turn me into some superhero if I kept up the showy miracles.

Moses: (*offended*) What's wrong with the showy miracles? Tap a rock, little water comes out, everybody listens to you, at least for a while.

Elijah: Plus, it's pretty fun when you have the power of God behind you. Shazam! Best. Sideshow. Ever.

Jesus: But I don't want to be a sideshow. I want to show them that they can do this stuff, too. It's not about killing off whoever believes something different.

Elijah: Hey!

Jesus: It's about living a life connected to God day by day, hour by hour, minute by minute.

Moses: Well, isn't that why God gave the Ten Commandments? To show people how to live?

Jesus: Yeah, but it's not all about the laws either. They've gone totally overboard on the law thing. Everything's either right or wrong. Mostly they figure, "What I think is right and what you think is wrong." (*touches the altar table*)

Elijah: Don't touch that, it's holy.

Jesus: (*rolls eyes*) Exactly what I mean. You start setting up laws and then everybody gets all excited about enforcing them. They forget the spirit of the law . . . the love that's behind them. It gets to be all about judgment and condemnation. Nobody needs that.

Peter: (*stumbling around a bit, while James and John still cower*) It is good for us to be here. I will make three dwellings so we can all live here happily ever after. (*aside*) Here let me get some plans together. (*pulls out a scroll*)

Narrator 1: What is this, Snow White?

James: Hey genius, what are you going to build that with?

John: And why do you have a scroll with you anyway?

Peter: This is a big deal! We should commemorate it somehow!

Narrator 1: Maybe a theme park?

Narrator 2: Or at least a historical marker?

John: You always want to build something.

James: But Jesus is always on the move. He never stays anywhere. Don't you remember . . . "Drop your nets and follow me"?

John: He's an on-the-go kind of guy.

Peter: But when things are important, you can't just let them pass by. You have to mark them.

James: With what, like a ceremony or something?

John: Start some kind of yearly ritual, like the Passover?

Peter: Now you're thinking.

Moses: (*shakes head*) Yep. Still don't get it.

Elijah: Lot of work to do there, my friend.

Jesus: (*sighs*) Why is it so hard for people to just follow God? To allow God's Spirit to direct their paths . . . to listen to the still small voice?

Elijah: That whole still small voice thing is pretty darn terrifying. Especially when it comes wrapped in hurricanes and earthquakes and stuff.

Moses: And burning bushes, and when it makes your face shine.

Narrator 1 and 2: (*sing*) Like a lightbulb.

Jesus: If you'd been listening better, God wouldn't have to do all that.

Elijah: So what are you going to do, Jesus?

Jesus: I'm heading into Jerusalem.

Moses: That's a whole world of trouble out there. They are not ready for you. Look at them.

James, John, and Peter are still fumbling around with the plans and trying to find things to build a shelter with. Peter manages to knock over everything.

John: Smooth.

Narrator 1 and 2: Epic failure.

Jesus: Perhaps not. People never seem to be ready when God calls on them. That's why only a few manage to be saints in their lifetime. You guys did it. (*They acknowledge this humbly.*) Who knows . . . maybe some of them will figure it out. I think Dad has big plans for Peter.

Elijah: That guy?

Moses: Good luck with that.

Elijah: Listen, Jesus, whatever you do . . . don't make the priests mad.

Moses: And don't make the people mad.

Elijah: And don't make the king mad . . . or the king's wife.

Jesus: The king was mad the day I was born. I think it kind of goes with the whole speaking-for-God territory. Well, thanks for the visit, friends.

Elijah: Any time.

Moses: See you real soon.

Jesus: That's what I'm afraid of.

Elijah and Moses step offstage.

Narrator 1: That's it? That's their big exit?

Narrator 2: Don't let the door hit you on your way out, prophet boy!

James: Wait. Where did they go?

John: Yeah, that was Moses. And Elijah! And I didn't even get to speak to them.

Narrator 1: Or get their autograph.

Narrator 2: And maybe sell it on eBay!

Peter: Didn't they like the plans I had for the cottages? I could've added some porches for a nice view.

James: It happened so fast.

John: Is this, like, holy ground now? Are we all gonna die? I don't want to die!

Jesus: Do not be afraid. (*as if it has just occurred to him*) In fact, keep silent about all of this. Tell no one until after the Son of Man had risen from the dead.

James: What's with you and the whole rising-from-the-dead thing?

John: Dead? Dude, you are supposed to be like Moses and Elijah. Elijah never died.

Peter: And Moses never . . . well, he never got into the Promised Land. But he lived a nice long life, wandering in the wilderness with the people Israel.

Jesus: (*sighs*) Come on, friends, let's head down the mountain.

Narrator 1: They'll be coming down the mountain when they come.

Narrator 2: Yee haw!

Peter: Seriously, why do you keep talking about dying? People don't want to hear that stuff.

James: I don't want to hear that stuff.

Peter: And the thing about being treated with contempt? We didn't sign onto this for contempt.

John: We want to be at your right hand!

James: And the left! When you establish your kingdom and all . . .

Peter: I could've made them a nice institution. We could have stained glass windows, and an altar, and put flowers on it, and stuff like that. It would last forever! People could come visit every Sunday, and . . .

Jesus shakes his head as they exit the sanctuary.

Narrator 1: Well, that's the end of our show.

Narrator 2: Nah, I bet there will be a cheesy sequel next year!

8

Week after Easter
Now What??

INTRODUCTION

IN THIS PLAY WE tackled one of the primary local church problems, the week-after-Easter let-down. We decided to work with all of the post-resurrection appearance-of-Jesus stories to create a play to be performed on the second Sunday of Easter, which traditionally uses the story about Thomas wanting to see the risen Lord for himself. As you engage the play, you will read some things that are probably heretical, such as likening the understanding imparted by Jesus and later by disciples through the power of the Holy Spirit to a Jedi mind trick. Cultural references such as the droning adult voice in Peanuts cartoons and Star Wars represent ways that the tweens tried to make sense of what is happening in these strange and wonderful Gospel stories.

Some might be concerned that this playfulness with these stories undercuts their sacred status. Can you do that with Scripture? But this frisky engagement represents a deeper form of questioning in younger adolescent form. Why didn't the disciples recognize Jesus after the resurrection? Why didn't they understand what he was trying to teach them? What is the power of the Holy Spirit, and how does it work? What is the power of the gospel in the face of an occupying empire? These are important theological questions for young people to engage. Their playfulness and ease with working with the stories comes from deep familiarity with them. And that is undoubtedly a good thing.

SCRIPTURE PASSAGES

Matthew 27:55—28:20; Luke 24; John 20–21

CHARACTERS

Jesus
Mary Magdalene
Mary, Mother of Somebody
Other Mary
Thomas
Peter
Cleopas
Howard, the unnamed disciple from the Emmaus road story
John
James

SCRIPT

In a simple room, behind locked doors, John, James, Peter, Cleopas, and Howard are hanging out in the room on couches. They look haggard and worn.

Peter: I still say those women are crazy. Someone just took his body to stir up trouble or something.

James: I know. What do they mean, "The body's not there. He has been raised"?

Peter: Now those guards are saying that we stole it. I think they're setting us up. (*He begins pacing around the room.*)

John: But what if they're right? (*turns to his brother*) If he's raised, I get to sit at his right hand, James.

James: No way, brother. Mom said I get the right hand.

John: The only right hand you're going to get is this one. (*shakes a fist at James*)

Peter: Will you two cut it out? There's not going to be any right hand. It's over. Finished. Jesus is *not* the Messiah.

James: You mean I'm not going to be the governor of Judea?

John: You were never going to be a regional governor. Sheesh.

Cleopas: Just a minute, Peter. It's not just the women. You know what Howard and I saw on the road to Emmaus.

Howard: Yeah. Jesus walked with us, and taught us about how he was the one from the Scriptures. Our hearts burned within us!

John: Well, it's a little hard to trust you guys. You didn't even recognize him for all the miles you were walking with him.

Cleopas: Well, he didn't look quite right. But as soon as he broke the bread, we knew it was him.

Howard: Yeah, he'd been all talk, talk, talk. The law . . . blah, blah, blah. The prophets . . . yak, yak, yak. Then, suddenly, it all made sense. Our hearts. Burning!

Peter: Yeah? Maybe your heartburn was caused by a little too much wine.

Cleopas: Was not!

James: Was too!

Their squabbling is interrupted by a knock on the door. All of them immediately get quiet and start trembling in fear, looking back and forth at one another. The three Marys are at the door. After they knock several times with no answer, they speak.

Mary Magdalene: (*impatiently*) Peter, come on, let us in.

Peter runs to the door, throws it open and looks worriedly around. He pulls the women in hurriedly, then shuts the door.

Peter: I thought I told you not to call me by my real name in public, Mary.

Mary Magdalene: (*rolling her eyes*) Peter, nobody is out there. What are you so scared of?

Peter: What am I scared of? I was nearly arrested. I had to fend them off three times on the night he was taken.

Other Mary: (*laughs derisively*) Fend them off? Yeah, you were real brave. You just denied you ever knew him.

Mary, Mother of Somebody: That's right, Other Mary. Three times before the cock crowed. Just like Jesus said.

Peter: Well, I didn't see anybody asking you if you were one of his followers.

Mary, Mother of Somebody: Well, occasionally it pays to be a woman. Means nobody takes you too seriously. They don't assume you are a follower of a radical threat to the entire religious establishment. "What about that woman?" "Oh, she's probably just somebody's mother."

Mary Magdalene: Or a prostitute.

Other Mary: Couldn't be one of the Twelve or anything like that. Just "some women" that followed him from Galilee.

James: Oh, come on. You know Jesus took you seriously. Now you're mad that the chief priests don't want your head on platter like John, Elizabeth's boy?

Mary Magdalene: No, we're not mad about that. We want you to listen to us. To take us seriously like Jesus did.

Other Mary: We know what we saw. And what the two shiny dudes told us.

Mary, Mother of Somebody: We're supposed to be heading back to Galilee, not hanging out here in a locked room like some ninnies.

Part II: Sample Dramas

The male disciples all begin protesting at once: "We're not ninnies!" "Hey! I don't want to be next!" "Nobody thinks you're any kind of threat," etc. While they are arguing, Jesus is suddenly among them. Howard sees him first, and looks like he's seen a ghost. Slowly, they all begin to notice him . . . falling out of chairs, cowering in corners, looking absolutely gobsmacked. Slowly they begin to recover.

Howard: Um, Jesus, right?

Cleopas: Are you a ghost? You can't be here.

Other Mary: We saw you crucified.

Mary, Mother of Somebody: Dead.

Mary Magdalene: Buried.

Peter: All our hopes that you were the One were crushed.

James: Yeah, you rode into Jerusalem on that donkey, and we could feel it happening.

Cleopas: Everyone was shouting and waving! "Hosanna!"

John: Then everyone was shouting again. "Crucify him!"

Jesus: Peace be with you.

All other characters: And also with you.

Mary Magdalene: (*warmly*) Your hands, your side. It is you, isn't it?

Jesus: In the flesh. (*looks at himself*) Well, more or less.

Howard: No, you must be a ghost.

Jesus: Howard, Howard. Here, give me some of that fish.

Howard shakes his head and backs away. James silently hands him a piece. Jesus takes it and eats it and makes a face.

Jesus: Ugh, Cleopas, have you been cooking again?

Peter: Rabbi, it *is* you!

Jesus: I thought we had covered that already. What are you doing here?

Other Mary: Hiding like a bunch of scared rabbits. They won't leave.

Mary, Mother of Somebody: Just sitting here behind locked doors.

John: Hey, they were locked. How did you get in here?

Howard: See, told you. He's a ghost!

Jesus: I'm not a ghost. I'm me. Only, different somehow.

Cleopas: I'll say. I hardly recognize you.

Mary Magdalene: Yeah. I thought you were the gardener at first. It's just so hard to believe you're here.

Other Mary: We saw you die.

Jesus: I know it's hard to understand, but don't you remember how I taught you? (*slips into Charlie Brown teacher voice*) The Scriptures . . . the Law . . . the Prophets.

Howard: See. It's happening again. I told you!

Jesus: Oh, right. (*makes Jedi mind trick sign and speaks more deliberately*) It all happened as it was foretold in the Scriptures.

Mary, Mother of Somebody: Oh! I remember. You told us you were going to go to Jerusalem.

James: And you were going to suffer and die.

John: But on the third day you were going to rise again (*getting excited and looking at his brother*) to sit at the right hand of the Father . . .

James: . . . and reign with him forever in eternal glory. John, Mom was right! (*They high five.*)

Jesus: Now, now, let's not get too excited. That reigning thing is not in the cards for you two.

James: You mean I'm still not going to get to be the governor of Judea?

Jesus: You were never going to get to be the governor of Judea. (*in the manner of a parent trying to get a small child excited about something they don't want to do*) No, no, you're going to the ends of the earth, to be my witnesses. Baptize, teach, heal. You know, like we'd already been doing.

Peter: Um, like you'd already been doing, Jesus. We were just kind of following along.

Cleopas: Yeah, not so much with the healing. I can't even cook fish.

Howard: Or the teaching. We couldn't even understand what you were saying, most of the time.

They all nod in agreement and talk all at once about how they never really got what he was doing, how they would have done it differently, etc.

Jesus: Um, hello. (*Jedi mind trick again*) Risen from the dead here?

All: (*acknowledging understanding*) Oh!

Mary Magdalene: I have to admit, that was pretty cool.

Howard: How do you do that? (*trying to do the Jedi mind trick move*)

Jesus: Power of the Holy Spirit. Don't worry, it's coming to you, too.

Mary, Mother of Somebody: (*doubtful*) But, you were crucified. Everybody thinks you were cursed, now.

Peter: How are we supposed to explain that one?

Cleopas: Or how you rode into Jerusalem for your big moment and managed to get killed within the week?

Other Mary: Or how to explain why your followers denied you ever existed and left you to die alone?

Mary Magdalene: And then hid in a room like some scared rabbits for the next few days?

The men all hang their heads.

Jesus: Now, now, it hasn't exactly been what anyone imagined when they thought about the Messiah returning.

James: I thought there would be more trumpets, less angry mobs.

Jesus: Exactly. But military overthrow of the Romans was not exactly what the Father had in mind, apparently.

John: Why not? Everybody hates the Romans.

Peter: That we could have explained. But what's our message now? Come, take up your cross and follow Jesus?

Jesus: Precisely. Good job, Peter! (*vanishes, or exits into the vestry*)

Peter: But, hey! Wait up! That's a terrible slogan.

Howard: That's not a mission, that's a death wish.

Cleopas: That's what we're supposed to teach? That doesn't make any kind of sense.

Mary Magdalene: When Jesus ate with sinners and hung out with a bunch of disreputable women, that didn't make any sense either. But I'm sure glad he did.

Mary, Mother of Somebody: You know, we were never quite clear on what he was up to.

John: And now we're supposed to be his witnesses? It'll never work.

Thomas comes in holding a sign: "One Week Later." He throws it off to the side.

Everyone: Thomas!

Thomas: Hi, friends. What's going on?

Other Mary: We're just trying to figure out what we're supposed to be doing.

Thomas: Doing? I thought we'd agreed to lay low for a little while. You know, try not to get killed?

Peter: That was the plan, at least until Jesus told us it was time to go be his witnesses.

Howard: He sent us to proclaim repentance and forgiveness of sins in his name to all nations.

Mary, Mother of Somebody: We have seen the Lord!

Thomas: Unless I see the mark of the nails in his hands, and put my finger in the mark of the nails and my hand in his side, I will not believe.

Everyone: Ew, that's gross! Disgusting!

Part II: Sample Dramas

While everyone is talking, Jesus appears again.

Cleopas: (*shouts in fright*) How do you keep doing that?

James: That door was locked!

Jesus: Peace be with you. (*They all settle down.*) Put your finger here, and see my hands. Reach out your hand and put it in my side. Do not doubt, but believe.

Thomas: (*falls to knees*) My Lord and my God!

Jesus: Have you believed because you have seen me? Blessed are those who have not seen and yet have come to believe.

Peter: Um, Jesus? About that. How are we going to get those who haven't seen you to believe us?

John: Yeah. Nobody is going to listen to us. Thomas didn't, and he'd been one of your followers for a long time.

Jesus: I'm sure you'll figure it out. Here, receive the Holy Spirit (*He breathes on them.*) Bye! (*He disappears.*)

Howard: Ooh, ooh. (*makes Jedi mind trick move*) Jesus is risen, indeed. (*looks around; then, as if deciding on his first victim, to Peter*) Your sins are forgiven.

Peter: What? (*shakes his head*) Enough of that now! We have work to do.

Howard: Holy Spirit, my Aunt Nancy. How did he do that? (*He keeps practicing.*)

Mary Magdalene: Don't you think it's time to leave our little hidey-hole and go to Galilee?

Cleopas: (*startled*) To Galilee? What are we going to do there?

Other Mary: To be witnesses? To proclaim repentance? You have the memory of a hamster.

John: Aren't you forgetting how hard it was for us to believe he was risen when you told us? How on earth are we supposed to get people to believe us?

James: We've got nothing but a dead guy and our story.

Mary, Mother of Somebody: And we can't get the story straight half the time.

Thomas: But Jesus was here. That's gotta count for something.

Peter: I think Mary is right.

Marys: Which one?

Peter: (*smiles*) Mary Magdalene. It's time to get out of here. Go out and tell the story. Step out in faith and hope we stay above the water.

Thomas: You know how well that worked the last time, Peter.

Peter starts pulling them out of chairs. Mary Magdalene helps. They slowly get up.

Peter: We've got this. Forgiveness of sins. People like the idea of grace.

Mary Magdalene: Eating with sinners. My personal favorite. Breaking bread together.

Other Mary: Telling stories. Parables to help people figure it out.

John: That's what we've got? Stories? Communion? Forgiveness? This is *so* not what I had in mind.

Cleopas: (*while exiting*) We've got that prayer, too. The one he taught us?

9

Pentecost
The Aftermath

INTRODUCTION

We had been doing plays for several years by the time we took on Pentecost, and many of the younger children wanted to be included in this one. The tweens felt great about that, and they wrote in the "Salted Fish" commercial interlude to include the younger siblings of the participants who wanted to be in the play. We also had a high school–aged German exchange student living with a family in the church who made her way in. The cameraman was a fifth-grader who didn't want to have to say any lines, so he was on stage throughout and did some physical humor additions but never spoke. The structure of the play really demonstrates how we were working with the tweens we had and the people they loved to include everyone.

The life resonance that the tweens found in this one is evident in the youthful imagination of what it must have been like to be drawn into a new religious movement. In Rachel the convert they wrote from their perspective about what it would feel like to worry what would happen if your parents found out you had joined a new religious movement. They laughed a bit at the miraculous actions that occurred in the story, linking speaking in tongues to Google Translate, and the cellophane tongues of flame provided a comedic moment. They had fun using the stock phrasing of reporters and conventions of news coverage completely out of place. At the same time, they used the voice of Peter to maintain a sense of potential awe at what was going on in the lives of the disciples in this signature moment in the birth of the Christian movement.

SCRIPTURE PASSAGE

Acts 2 and Joel 2:28–32

CHARACTERS

Reporter (uses own name)
James
John
Verena, a German-speaking visitor
Peter/Google Translator
Jerusalemite
Matthias
Rachel the convert
Cameraperson

SCRIPT

We began this play with a brief, mime-like re-enactment of Pentecost, using sound clips of fire crackling, rushing wind, and babbling languages. All of the characters except for the reporter and cameraperson participated, using simple props like headbands with cellophane flames attached to create a comical version of the story.

Reporter: Are we on?

Part II: Sample Dramas

Camaraperson nods vigorously.

Reporter: This is [actor's name], with Channel 7 Jerusalem. I'm here on the scene of the aftermath of Pentecost with live coverage to keep you informed. Earlier today, an entire crowd of people had gathered for the feast of Pentecost when some kind of explosion occurred just over there. (*points to area where mime occurred*) Some are calling it a group delusion, others the birth of some weird cult, with witnesses reporting what they called a great rush of wind. Some even spoke of tongues of flame that seemed to descend on their heads. Then there was some kind of confused speech event, where people reportedly heard a group of Galileans speaking in the tongues of several other nations. (*pauses for a moment, pressing an imaginary earpiece to head, as if listening*) It does sound strange, Jim. A group of local young men and women were able to deliver a message understood by people from Crete, Mesopotamia, even Egypt. Let's go speak to some of the eyewitnesses on the scene. (*turns to Verena*) This is Verena, a visitor to Jerusalem from the territories north of Rome.

Verena: (*excitedly in German*) We were all just sitting around, and then "whoosh" and then "aah."

Google Translator: We were all just sitting around, and then "whoosh" and then "aah."

Reporter: You obviously aren't from around here. Why were you here in Jerusalem?

Verena: (*still in German*) I'm here for Pentecost. Nobody else has been able to speak my language since I got here. Then these locals had . . . I'm not sure how to explain it . . . but tongues of flame on their heads. They started speaking German, and I understood.

Google Translator: I'm here for Pentecost. Nobody else has been able to speak my language since I got here. Then these locals had— how do you say it?—tomatoes on their head. They started speaking German, and I understood.

Reporter: Thank you so much. (*walks away a bit*) Jim, I think we might have translation issues in that interview. Other sources have been saying they saw tongues of flame descend. (*Verena looks indignantly at Google Translator, who shrugs.*) Let's check in with another witness. Excuse me, ma'am, you are from Jerusalem. Can you tell us what happened this morning?

Jerusalemite: Bunch of crazy people, partying all night.

Reporter: So, you dispute their account?

Jerusalemite: I still say this is nothing but the booze talking.

Reporter: So, you believe that this entire crowd of people was intoxicated at 9 a.m., and that was the source of some kind of mass delusion?

Jerusalemite: Well, it weren't no delusion. There was a big blow and some little sparky thingies in the air. But all of that chatter just made me a little crazy. Something about this dude Jesus, and how he's the Messiah who will bring us salvation. Bunch of hooey if you ask me.

Reporter: Thank you, ma'am. (*walks away from her*) Let's get a little closer, Jim. Ah yes, here we have two of the insiders, some Galilean brothers, James and John. Thanks for speaking with us today.

James and John: Sure.

Reporter: You are followers of a carpenter's son, named Jeebus, correct?

James: Jesus.

Reporter: Excuse me?

James: His name was Jesus.

Reporter: Right. And is this Jesus in the crowd today?

John: (*looking sad*) No, he was killed just a few weeks ago.

Reporter: Oh, I am sorry for your loss. So who was leading your group today?

James: (*smiling*) Well, believe it or not, it was Peter.

Reporter: (*disbelieving*) A rock was in charge of all of this?

John: No, a man named Peter. He's a friend of ours.

James: Not always very reliable, but today he came through.

Reporter: Is he the one who was rumored to give a big speech?

James: That's right. Filled with the Holy Spirit, he was on fire today.

John: Well, not literally. Umm, we did have flames on our heads. It's kind of hard to explain.

Reporter: Yes, I'm getting a lot of that.

James: Anyway, when Peter stood up to try to explain it, we knew we were in trouble.

John: Yeah, in the past, he denied Jesus more than he really proclaimed him.

James: He's had some pretty major missteps.

James and John: (*to each other*) Yeah, remember when he got out of the boat? (*They mime Peter walking and splashing, and tell it to each other like an inside joke.*)

Reporter: And?

John: Today, he really broke it down for the crowd. Stood up and gave a great speech.

James: When Jesus died, we felt really lost. We gave up everything to follow him, and then he went and got himself crucified.

John: Then there was the whole resurrection thing, and that was great. But, he left us again.

James: Yeah, ascended into heaven and left us standing there. We didn't know who we were going to follow.

John: And now we have followers! Crazy!

James: We've been given the Holy Spirit, and we're the leaders.

John: Power from on high. Power to heal and to teach. It's kind of weird.

James: But pretty cool at the same time. Kind of like when Harry Potter figured out he was a wizard.

Matthias runs across the stage, slapping at his hair.

Matthias: (*yelling in panic*) I'm on fire! Is it still there? I didn't sign up for this!

Reporter: Who was that?

John and James sigh and shake their heads.

James: Matthias.

John: New guy.

Reporter: Were you recruiting?

James: We lost one of our group when Jesus died, so we had to replace him. Now we have all kinds of people wanting to follow Jesus.

Reporter: In fact, we have one to interview right now. Thank you, James and John. Before we continue, a word from our sponsors.

Two older children and several smaller children come across the stage. The older children are playing parents. The younger children are dragging their heels and whining to their parents. One of the tweens sings the little jingle while the older children stop, pull out some snack crackers, and feed them to the younger children. The young children immediately perk up and skip the rest of the way across the stage.

On a journey? Need a snack?

Try salted fish, the snack that smiles back. Salt Fish!

The older children playing the parents exit the stage.

Reporter: Could you tell us your name?

James and John leave. Rachel arrives.

Rachel: I'm Rachel.

Reporter: And were you a follow of this Jesus?

Rachel: No, I had heard that a teacher had been arrested and killed. But I wasn't a part of all that.

Reporter: Did you see what happened?

Rachel: I heard the sound, and came out to see what was going on. It was pretty chaotic until Peter stood up to speak.

Reporter: What did he say?

Rachel: He talked about the prophet Joel, and explained that this Spirit was the same one he talked about. Now is the day of the Lord, when the Messiah is made known to us.

Reporter: Wait a minute. You mean this Jesus is supposed to be the Messiah?

Rachel: That's what Peter said. And he and the others were filled with amazing power. So I was baptized, and joined them.

Reporter: And what do your parents think about this decision?

Rachel: (*sheepish*) I haven't exactly told them yet.

Reporter: Do you think they might be angry that you are going against tradition?

Rachel: I think I'm actually following the tradition. Like Peter said, Jesus is fulfilling the words of the prophets.

Reporter: It seems like a lot of the other Jews in Jerusalem may not be convinced that this teacher is the Messiah.

Rachel: They just haven't experienced what's going on here. Nearly three thousand of us felt the Spirit today and were baptized.

Reporter: It sounds like quite an experience. Thank you for talking with us today. (*walks away from Rachel*) Now we have an exclusive interview with Peter, a former fisherman who seems to be in charge of this group. Here he is now. (*as Peter walks up*) Thank you for taking the time to speak with us, Peter.

Peter: I'm glad to be here with you, [reporter's name]. Honored to witness to the Spirit's power.

Reporter: What is this Spirit that you are speaking of? Is it some sort of demonic possession? Or the kind of "spirit" that emerges from a jug after a short period of fermentation?

Peter: No, no, nothing like that. What happened today was an outpouring of the Holy Spirit, from God. Jesus said it would come to us.

Reporter: And this Spirit performs pyrotechnics, and makes people speak in tongues?

Peter: I think the wind and flame was just to get our attention, so that probably won't happen again. The real work of the Spirit is to create understanding and connection, the ability to hear and actually understand each other, even when we're really quite different.

Reporter: And what about the masses coming to get baptized, and joining this cult of yours?

Peter: (*shaking his head and waving his hands a bit*) Not my cult. We are simply worshiping the God of Jacob, the God of our ancestors. But today we have experienced something special: the outpouring of the Spirit that was spoken of in the prophets, like in Joel, where he says the young men shall have visions and the young women shall dream dreams.

Reporter: And these dreams make these young people leave their homes, join this group in the breaking of bread, listen to your teaching, even share their possessions?

Peter: Jesus reminded us that the way of life is loving the Lord our God with all our heart, mind, soul, and strength, and loving our neighbors as ourselves. What we have here today (*uses his arms to indicate the congregation*) is a group of people who have been called out to live that in their everyday lives, together.

Reporter: (*a little disappointed*) That doesn't sound like much.

Peter: (*smiling*) You'd be surprised how difficult it is, sometimes. But we have the Spirit to bring us together, and it gives us the power to love and to heal, to share one another's joys and burdens.

Reporter: What does this deceased rabbi, Jesus, have to do with all of it?

Peter: Oh, he's not dead.

Part II: Sample Dramas

Reporter: (*looking around*) So, he's here in the crowd today?

Peter: Yes and no. It's a little complicated.

Reporter: (*a little exasperated*) So I hear.

Peter: When people are baptized in Jesus' name, they receive forgiveness and the gift of the Holy Spirit. The Spirit gives them the power to love with God's love. They feel cleansed and renewed, ready to go out into the world with gladness to love and serve their neighbors.

Reporter: Okay (*obviously not getting it*). Well, thank you for serving as a witness to this event today.

Peter: My pleasure. (*He walks off.*)

Reporter: Well, Jim, that about wraps it up. Was it an outpouring of the Spirit? Or too much partying? You've heard the eyewitness accounts. Will these followers of Jesus continue to add to their number? We'll just have to wait and see. This is [reporter's name], reporting for Channel 7 Jerusalem. Holy news for a holy city.

10

Writing Jonah

INTRODUCTION

HERE IS AN EXAMPLE of a play written about a single character from the Bible, Jonah. As we studied the book of Jonah, we learned that it is one of the most literary pieces in the Bible, clearly designed for the written form. As we read the story, the tweens became curious about why someone would go to the trouble to write a story about a prophet but then make him sound like such a loser. That feeling worked its way into the frame of the story, which became about the writer of Jonah arguing with an editor about the story he was creating. This allowed the tweens to let their voice be the voice of the editor, inserting their questions about the story into the play through the voice of the editor.

One of my favorite parts about this play is that it embodies the classic tween struggle of coming to terms with their emerging scientific reasoning skills and what to do with a farcical fairy tale like the book of Jonah in light of it. Here, the tweens included both their interest that the use of the term "whale" is not a great translation of the Hebrew term for the fish in the story and their scientific reasoning in a great speech by the editor, which was actually written by a member of the class. In it, the editor muses about what species of whale would have been able to eat a human,

Part II: Sample Dramas

what the pH level of a whale's stomach would be, and the reality that a whale's dives might cause the bends in a human being. In this speech, they were able to give voice to the doubts and questions raised about the literal truthfulness of the story. The framing presence of the human author and editor point to their emerging sophistication about the input of human hands in the process of creating the Bible.

You can also see their brainstorming about who would be as evil a villain to our congregation as the people of Ninevah would have been to the original audience of Jonah, which led to contemporary connections with Westboro Baptist and ISIS. The great spaghetti monster was this play's inside joke with the tweens. At this point, I'm not sure any of us could recreate the origins of the spaghetti monster conversation, but it had something to do with the religions lost to time and history that would have been the religions of the sailors on the boat. They insisted that we keep it in, so we had to work around it. The magic eight ball was the tween translation of casting lots, since we never could find out exactly the mechanism for doing that, which would have been in effect in Jonah's time.

This is one of the few plays that we have constructed that draws directly on the reception history of the text. Early Christians recognized the resonances of Jesus' death and resurrection in the three days that Jonah spent in the belly of the whale. Did you know that there are more images of Jonah than Jesus in early Christian catacombs? This was one of the things we discovered in our exploration of how and why Jonah remained important to our religious ancestors, and we tried to work that discovery into the play. But we also wanted to work in that they had wrestled with what it meant to collapse the story of Jonah and Jesus and in history.

SCRIPTURAL PASSAGE

Jonah 1–4

CHARACTERS

Writer (we used the actor's actual name in the play, here Kieran)
Editor (actor's name again, here Megan)
Jonah
Sailor 1
Sailor 2
Extra Sailors, Bird, Whale, Messenger Child, and Repenting Animals (played by younger elementary children who wanted to be included in our play)

STAGING

The writer and editor stood at lecterns to the side of the stage and read the script while other characters acted out the story in the center part of the stage. This show required more props than many of the others. We acquired appliance boxes and made a cardboard whale and a boat shape out of them, which we used in rudimentary ways in the show. The boat was carried at all times by a sailor or two, for example. The whale was played by two elementary school–aged children who carried it onstage and used it to hide Jonah's body and later to "spit" him out. The sailors wore pirate hats made from folded newspaper, and Jonah had "Jonah" written on his t-shirt to identify him. We borrowed Halloween animal costumes for the children and used pieces of burlap with a neck cut and a rope waist. Otherwise all characters were wearing whatever they wore to church that day.

SCRIPT

Writer: So, Kieran, I've been telling you about this book I've been writing about the prophet Jonah.

Editor: Sure, Megan. You know, we don't hear much about Jonah, so I'm glad that you are filling in the details a little bit.

Writer: I've been through several drafts. So, you know how we've talked about how all the great early biblical prophets have cool stories about them . . .

Editor: Like Moses and the bulrushes and the pillar of fire and all that?

Writer: Right.

Editor: Sure. So what's Jonah's story?

Writer: How about I just read it, and you can help me make it better?

Editor: So, just interrupt if I have any comments?

Writer: Well, within reason, I suppose.

Editor: Of course. I'll keep my commentary to a minimum. Go ahead.

Writer: Now the word of the Lord came to Jonah son of Amittai, saying . . .

Jonah enters and walks to center stage as soon as the writer starts the story. Someone off to the side throws a wadded up paper ball at Jonah's head, who picks it up and unfolds the note to read it.

Editor: So *how* did the word of the Lord come to Jonah? That seems like an important detail.

Writer: I don't know, maybe it was in a dream or something like that.

Jonah drops to the ground and begins to snore.

Editor: Well, the other books of the Bible are kind of explicit on that point, right? There's a vision, or a burning bush, or angels show up. I know! How about a text?

Jonah's phone makes a pinging sound as he rolls to his feet, and he pulls it out to look at it.

Writer: God *texts* now?

Editor: Well, it would be an easy way to talk to people. But, a little hard to believe, I guess. Kind of obvious. How about a little bird comes to Jonah and whispers it in his ear . . .

Jonah puts the phone away, and then another little kid dressed like a bird starts to come "flying" in from the side here until the action is interrupted by the writer.

Writer: (*as if speaking to a small child*) How about we leave it at "The word of the Lord came to Jonah" and the reader can imagine how that might have happened.

Little kid backs away slowly to the side.

Editor: But don't you think . . . (*stops mid-sentence when the Writer glares at him*) Okay, sorry. Vague might be best. Continue.

Writer: The word of the Lord came to Jonah, son of Amittai, saying, "Go at once to Nineveh, that great city, and cry out against it; for their wickedness has come up before me."

Editor: Ooh, what did they do?

Writer: Who?

Editor: The Ninevites? You've got to let your readers hear the dirt! All the juicy details! Wickedness sells, my friend.

Writer: Everyone knows about the people of Nineveh. They sent soldiers to invade and kill us Israelites. Twice!

Editor: But that was a long time ago. You need to make it more immediate for your reader.

Writer: Well, Nineveh is kind of a stock villain here. People can translate it into their own enemies.

Editor: But, if you made it specific to something more recent, they'd get the point, like . . . I know! The word of the Lord came to Jonah and said, "Go to Westboro Baptist and tell Fred Phelps . . ."

Jonah looks with horror at the editor.

Editor: (*pointing to Jonah*) See, that got his attention. Or, the word of the Lord said, "Go to Raqqa, Syria."

Part II: Sample Dramas

Writer: Raqqa, Syria?

Editor: You know, home base for ISIS?

Writer: Look, I'm going for timeless here. Everybody knows that Nineveh means whatever big, bad enemy people have. It's a metaphor.

Jonah starts tapping his foot impatiently.

Editor: But if you . . .

Writer: Look, we are never going to get through this if you keep arguing with me. I'm leaving it at Nineveh for now.

Editor: Fine.

Writer: So, where were we? Oh right. But Jonah set out to flee to Tarshish from the presence of the Lord.

Jonah exits stage.

Editor: (*laughing*) Flee the presence of the Lord? That's like saying, "He stepped out of the sanctuary before he beat up his brother so God wouldn't see him do it."

Writer: Of course. The presence of the Lord is everywhere. But sometimes people start to think that God can only be in one place. Like church. Or the mountains. Or Jerusalem. I'm kind of making fun of Jonah.

Editor: But I thought you were writing this to give Jonah a good backstory.

Jonah and sailors come out in boat. They mimic getting tossed about in a boat and scared.

Writer: Just go with me. So anyway, Jonah got on the boat in the complete opposite direction from where God told him to go, so the ship started to experience a storm.

Editor: Ooh, that's good. A storm at sea.

Writer: The sailors were very afraid, and each one cried out to their own gods.

Sailors step in front of boat and mimic meditation poses, bowing in full prostration, begging and pleading.

Sailor 1: Oh great Spaghetti Monster, come to me in your great giant peach and carry me to your all-you-can-eat buffet!

Sailor 2: You and your stupid Spaghetti Monster!

Sailors return to boat.

Editor: Umm . . . Spaghetti Monster? What have you been reading, anyway? Roald Dahl? Wouldn't the sailors have been Assyrians and Egyptians and people like that?

Writer: The point is that they had their own gods, but later they show more faith in Jonah's god than even Jonah does.

Editor: I feel like you may be making fun of their religions.

Jonah lays down.

Writer: Okay, I'll cut that part. Jonah, meanwhile, had gone down into the hold of the ship, laid down, and was fast asleep.

Editor: Ooh, like Jesus in that story with the disciples.

Writer: Hasn't been written yet. Different religion, comes later.

Editor: Oh, right.

Writer: So the captain said to Jonah, "What are you doing sound asleep? Call on your God!" Meanwhile, the sailors decided to cast lots to figure out who was to blame for the calamity.

Sailors consult a magic eight ball, then point to Jonah.

Writer: When they found out he was a Hebrew who worshipped the Lord, the God of heaven, they were doubly scared. They said to him, "What is this that you have done!" For they knew that he was fleeing from the presence of the Lord.

Editor: How did they know that?

Writer: I don't know. Maybe he told them.

Editor: Then say that.

Writer nods and makes a note.

Writer: The sailors asked what they should do to get the sea to calm down, and Jonah said, "Throw me overboard."

Jonah mimics tossing someone overboard. Sailors look horrified. They refuse and start rowing harder, but the sea becomes even stormier.

The sailors cried out to Jonah's God, "Please, O Lord, we pray, do not let us perish on account of this man's life. Do not make us guilty of this man's life."

Editor: Wait, I thought that they believed in other gods.

Writer: They do.

Editor: So why are they talking to Jonah's God now?

Writer: Well, it's irony. Jonah is supposed to be this big prophet, right? But these heathen sailors trust in his God's power more than he does.

Editor: Oh. So what happens next?

Writer: They threw Jonah overboard, and then made a sacrifice to the Lord because of their actions.

Sailors toss him overboard and exit. Jonah swims for a minute.

Editor: How was that supposed to fix things?

Writer: Well, I guess they weren't enabling him, anyway.

Editor: This is getting weird.

Whale enters from the other side and begins to swallow Jonah as next line happens.

Writer: Then the Lord provided a large fish to swallow up Jonah, where he stayed for three days and three nights.

Editor: Like Jesus!

Writer: Again, hasn't happened yet. Different book, different religion, remember?

Editor: But, c'mon. Three days and three nights? In a dark place?

Writer: That will be a tomb. This is a big fish.

Editor: Wait, what? A fish? Do you mean a whale?

Writer: Did I *say* "whale"?

Editor: But, that's so vague. A big fish could be anything from a whale shark to a freakishly large raccoon butterfly fish. At least a whale gives you some idea of what we're dealing with.

Writer: Fine. (*makes a big show of crossing it out*) Whale.

Editor: But then, is it a baleen whale or a toothed whale? Because I could understand a toothed whale, but unless there's some mystical size-changing stuff going on, you can't fit between the fibers in a baleen plate. And then, is there air in a whale's inside? And if the whale dove down, wouldn't he get the bends? I don't know about you, but I don't think Jonah would make it if his blood got carbonated. Is he getting swallowed? Hydrochloric acid has a pH of 1.5–3.5 in the stomach. Also, wouldn't he be crushed by . . .

Writer: You have no problem with the fact that my character just got picked up by a . . . a sea creature of some sort, but you freak out over the fact that he might be swallowed?

Editor: Well, if you think about it, there's no way that could have happened.

Writer: All right, Mr. Neil deGrasse Tyson. It's a story, not a scientific treatise. The point is that God has the power to make things happen. Then Jonah prayed to the Lord his God from the belly of the fish, saying:

Jonah: (*to the tune of John Denver's "Leaving on a Jet Plane"*) Cause I'm living in a big whale,

Don't know why I'm in this weird tale,

O God, don't make me go.

Editor: (*makes a huge face*) Um, that doesn't sound like a faithful prayer. Too bouncy. Maybe something a little more formal?

Writer: Okay, okay. Let's try this:

Jonah: (*to the tune of the Beatles' "Yesterday"*) Yesterday, all my troubles seemed so far away,

A whale swallowed me and I'm here to stay,

Part II: Sample Dramas

O God, please let me run away.

Editor: This is a prophet of God. Don't you think it would sound more like a psalm or something? Not this popular junk.

Writer: I was trying to spice it up a bit, but fine.

He makes a big show out of erasing the manuscript and writing again, while Jonah very formally kneels, puts his hands together, and recites:

Jonah: "I called to the Lord out of my distress, and he answered me,

out of the belly of Sheol I cried, and you heard my voice.

You cast me into the deep in the the heart of the seas, and the flood surrounded me;

all your waves and your billows passed over me."

Editor: Ooh, that's good. That sounds just like a psalm. Did you get it from there?

Writer: No, but I'll take that as a compliment. Anyway, I'll keep heading in that direction and finish it later. So then the Lord spoke to the fish, and it spewed Jonah onto dry land.

Jonah jumps out from behind the cardboard whale.

Editor: Ew!

Writer: Now what?

Editor: That. Is. Disgusting.

Writer: Well, how else would he get out of the belly of the big fish?

They both think about this for a moment, while Jonah and the other characters look at each other and at the whale.

Editor: Moving on.

Writer: The word of the Lord came to Jonah again . . .

One of the little kids scooters down the main aisle of the church, tugs hard on Jonah's leg, and hands him a note. Jonah opens the note.

Any comments about that?

Editor: Nope.

Writer: Saying, "Get up, go to Nineveh, that great city, and proclaim to it the message that I tell you." It was a big city, three days' walk across, and Jonah began to cry out:

Jonah crosses the stage with a different sign each time the Writer says one of the phrases in quotation marks below. We used cardboard and a yardstick to mimic a protestor's sign, with the final sign simply containing a picture of the face of Santa Claus rather than the song lyrics.

"Quit screwing around and behave yourselves."

Editor: Um, Megan, I don't think God would talk like that.

Writer: Maybe a little too much like an angry parent. How about:

"You're going to die. You are all going to die!"

Editor: No warning, no chance to repent?

Writer: How about:

"He sees you when you're sleeping, he knows when you're awake. He knows if you've been bad or good, so be good for goodness' sake."

Editor: Is God some kind of stalker or something? That's too creepy.

Writer: True. How about:

"Forty days more, and Nineveh shall be overthrown!"

Editor: A little vague, but better than the other ones.

Jonah exits.

Writer: And the people of Nineveh believed God, they proclaimed a fast, and everyone, great and small, put on sackcloth.

Editor: Doesn't that seem, well, a little abrupt? I mean, it's not like these horrible evildoers are going to just do what God says right away.

Writer: Again with the irony. The prophet won't listen to God, but the sailors, the Ninevites, everyone who you don't expect to be faithful, is!

Editor: That seems a little hard to believe. Like, God could redeem terrorists? Or horrible bigots? Or people who text at the theater?

Writer: That's the whole point. Even our enemies are beloved by God. If they respond to God's call, God will save them.

Editor: But even when King David repented with sackcloth and ashes, God didn't change his mind. Why would he for the terrible Ninevites?

Writer: That's my whole point. I don't like that part of the David story. God does respond to the actions of humans. If a whole city repented, God wouldn't destroy them.

Editor: Well, you would need to make their repentance even better than King David's after that whole Bathsheba thing.

Writer: Okay, how about the king of Nineveh declares that even the animals have to fast and wear sackcloth?

Editor: The animals? That seems a little ridiculous.

Some of the little children enter from the vestry, dressed as animals and covered in burlap. The editor gestures at them.

I mean, really. No one is going to believe that the animals didn't eat and wore burlap and ashes.

Writer: You were the one who said that it needed to be something more impressive than regular repentance. You got a better idea?

Editor: (*thinking*) No. But that makes this whole thing seem like a fairy tale.

Writer: So, you were with me through the whole swallowed-by-a-big-fish thing, but you're worried about the animals repenting?

Editor: Have you ever tried to force a cat into a sack? That's even more ridiculous than being sucked through baleen.

Writer: So then God saw their acts of repentance and declared that they would not experience disaster.

Editor: I still think someone as bad as the people of Nineveh wouldn't change their mind that quickly.

Writer: You sound like Jonah. He gets so mad that he starts asking God to kill him already throughout the end of this story.

Editor: Have you written that part yet?

Writer: I haven't finished exactly, but Jonah's gonna be irritated at God's show of mercy.

Editor: So what's Jonah gonna learn at the end?

Writer: He has to learn something?

Editor: Isn't he supposed to be a prophet? Doesn't he turn his life around and become a great leader?

Writer: No, it's done. I think I've made my point.

Editor: But I thought you were trying to let people know who Jonah was and why he was important.

Writer: Prophets, they're just like us.

Editor: That's never going to get in the Bible. (*walks off*)

Bibliography

Bushnell, Horace. *Building Eras in Religion.* New York: Scribner's, 1881.
Cassian, John. *Conferences.* Translated by Colm Luibheid. Classics of Western Spirituality. New York: Paulist, 1985.
Erikson, Erik H. *Insight and Responsibility.* New York: Norton, 1964.
Foster, Charles R. *Educating Congregations: The Future of Christian Education.* Nashville: Abingdon, 1994.
Fowler, James W. "Gifting the Imagination: Awakening and Informing Children's Faith." *Review and Expositor* 80 (1982) 189–200.
———. *Stages of Faith: The Psychology of Human Development and the Quest for Meaning.* New York: Harper Collins, 1981.
Martin, Dale B. *Pedagogy of the Bible: An Analysis and a Proposal.* Louisville: Westminster John Knox, 2008.
Nakkula, Michael J., and Eric Toshalis. *Understanding Youth: Adolescent Development for Educators.* Cambridge, MA: Harvard Educational, 2006.
Nye, Rebecca. *Children's Spirituality: What It Is and Why It Matters.* London: Church House, 2009.
O'Connor, Kathleen M. "Crossing Borders: Biblical Studies in a Trans-Cultural World." In *Teaching the Bible: The Discourses and Politics of Biblical Pedagogy,* edited by Fernando F. Segovia and Mary Ann Tolbert, 322–37. Maryknoll, NY: Orbis, 1998.
Parks, Sharon Daloz. *Big Questions, Worthy Dreams: Mentoring Emerging Adults in Their Search for Meaning, Purpose, and Faith.* 2nd ed. San Francisco: Jossey-Bass, 2011.
Sasso, Sandy Eisenberg. *God's Echo: Exploring Scripture with Midrash.* Brewster, MA: Paraclete, 2007.
———. *Noah's Wife: The Story of Naamah.* Illustrated by Bethanne Andersen. Nashville: Jewish Lights, 2002.
Smith, Christian, and Melinda Lundquist Denton. *Soul Searching: The Religious and Spiritual Lives of American Teenagers.* New York: Oxford University Press, 2009.
Strauch, Barbara. *The Primal Teen: What the New Discoveries about the Teenage Brain Tell Us about Our Kids.* New York: Anchor, 2004.

BIBLIOGRAPHY

Throckmorton, Burton H. *Gospel Parallels: A Comparison of the Synoptic Gospels.* 5th ed. Nashville: T. Nelson, 1992.

Warren, Michael. *At This Time, in This Place: The Spirit Embodied in the Local Assembly.* Harrisburg, PA: Trinity, 1999.

www.ingramcontent.com/pod-product-compliance
Lightning Source LLC
Chambersburg PA
CBHW070929160426
43193CB00011B/1630